THAT CHAMPIONSHIP SEASON

The 1995 Northwestern Wildcats' Road to the Rose Bowl

Edited by
FRANCIS J. FITZGERALD

Introduction by
OTTO GRAHAM

Louisville, Kentucky

Acknowledgments

Research assistance: Jim Russ, Matt Rennie and Karen Van Antwerp, *The Detroit News*; Susan Quigley and the Harold Washington Library Center, Chicago, Ill.; Pat Harmon, College Football Hall of Fame; Tom Gilbert, Wide World Photos; Jamie Calsyn, Allsport; Norm Goldstein, The Associated Press; Jim Willis, *The Birmingham Post-Herald*; Seija Schiff, *The New York Times*; Lupe Salazar, *The Los Angeles Times*; Tom Hardin, *The Detroit News*, and Brad Hurlbut and the Northwestern University Sports Information Office.

Copyright © 1996 by AdCraft Sports Marketing.

No part of this work covered by the copyright hereon may be reproduced or used in any form or by any means graphic, electronic, or mechanical, including photographing, recording, taping, or in information storage and retrieval systems without the permission of the publisher.

ISBN 1-887761-02-0
Library of Congress Catalog Card Number: 95-83850

Cover and Book Design by Chris Kozlowski
Typeface: Kis-Janson

PUBLISHED BY:
AdCraft Sports Marketing
Kaden Tower, 10th Floor
6100 Dutchmans Lane
Louisville, KY 40205
(502) 473-1124

"It was because you do not have enough faith," answered Jesus.
"Remember this!
If you have faith as big as a mustard seed,
you can say to the hill, 'Go from here to there' and it will go.
You can do anything!"

— Matthew 17:20

Contents

Introduction by Otto Graham VII

1. Year of the Cats 9

2. Cats Shock Irish 17
   Northwestern vs. Notre Dame, September 2, 1995

3. Dashed Dreams 29
   Northwestern vs. Miami (Ohio), September 16, 1995

4. High-Flying Cats 35
   Northwestern vs. Air Force, September 23, 1995

5. Northwestern Routs Hoosiers 41
   Northwestern vs. Indiana, September 30, 1995

6. The Miracle Worker 51
   Northwestern's Gary Barnett

7. Stopping a Giant 57
   Northwestern vs. Michigan, October 7, 1995

8. The New Guys on the Block 73
   Northwestern vs. Minnesota, October 14, 1995

9. A Badger Bash 79
   Northwestern vs. Wisconsin, October 21, 1995

10. Valiant Comeback 89
    Northwestern vs. Illinois, October 28, 1995

11. Cats Continue to Roll 97
    Northwestern vs. Penn State, November 4, 1995

12. Dreaming of Roses 113
    Northwestern vs. Iowa, November 11, 1995

13. Champions, Finally 121
    Northwestern vs. Purdue, November 18, 1995

14. Purple Craze 131
    Northwestern Hysteria Spreads Beyond Chicago

15. A Knight on the Field 141
    Darnell Autry leads NU to Greatness

16. The Purple to Pasadena 145
    Northwestern vs. Southern California, January 1, 1996

Appendix 157

INTRODUCTION

On the shores of Lake Michigan is one of the most beautiful schools in America: Northwestern University. It is unusual in the sense that it offers the highest ideals for its students; the perfection that can be required only in a truly great university. These high expectations cause many hopeful high school students to fall by the wayside because of not having high enough class standings or enough extra curricular activities to satisfy entrance requirements.

What an honor it was to be accepted to this great school. I question whether or not I would have been selected by today's standards. It is an even greater honor to graduate from this fine institution knowing that you have given 100 percent for four years and have beaten the odds.

Northwestern can give you any kind of education you desire from the theater, medicine, law, journalism or the ability to design tall buildings. Because of Northwestern's selective admission standards, the student body is well diversified; and the school offers a multi-faceted curriculum. Evanston — being so close to Chicago — gives the student a unique enrichment of opportunities.

I was fortunate to receive a basketball scholarship to Northwestern in 1939, which I dearly needed since both my parents were school teachers and could not afford to send me to such a prestigious school. I had to decide between Dartmouth and NU. However, because of the fine recruiting of the assistant athletic director, Ade Schumacher, I could see the advantage of going to a school near my home in Waukegan, Ill., and yet far enough away to offer me a feeling of independence. Many of my lifetime friendships were formed at my fraternity and on my respective athletic teams. My football career at Northwestern started in earnest when I was "discovered" playing intramural football and Pappy Waldorf asked me to try out for the team. The rest is history.

One day last year, the Northwestern alumni of Sarasota, Fla., invited Wildcats athletic director Rick Taylor and Gary Barnett, our football coach, to visit with us. They were an impressive pair. They told us of their future plans for the athletic program, including

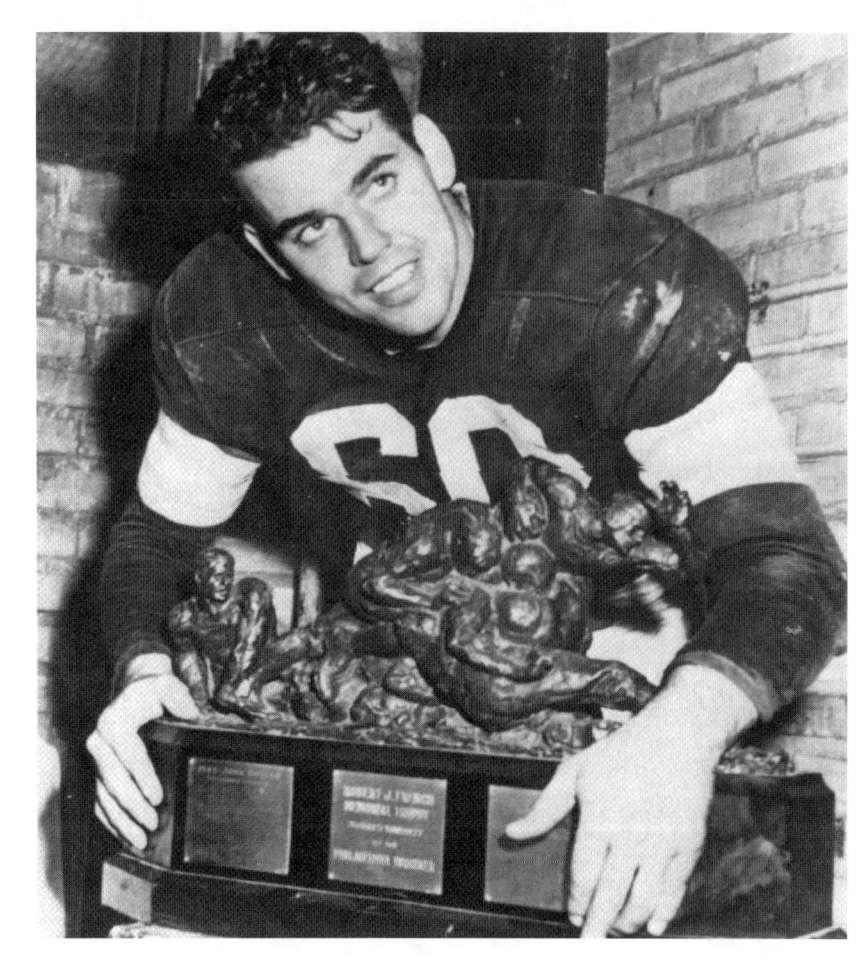

how they would continue to recruit quality athletes who were quality people, yet would not sacrifice Northwestern's high academic standards. Their vision was a gutsy one, considering the track record of the many others who had chartered a similar course. And, now, that dream is coming true.

Over the past four years, Gary Barnett and his coaching staff have brought a new way of thinking to Northwestern. They weren't afraid to challenge the football team's past tradition of gridiron mediocrity. In the end, they not only changed that tradition, but also changed the attitudes of an entire football program, a university and, perhaps, the way the country now views Northwestern football.

This book, *That Championship Season: The 1995 Northwestern Wildcats' Road to the Rose Bowl*, chronicles that special story. From NU's biggest win ever against Notre Dame at the beginning of the season, to the Rose Bowl, *That Championship Season* brings to life Northwestern's journey to Pasadena and its date with destiny.

Speaking for all Northwestern alums, we are very proud of the accomplishments of the 1995 Wildcats. Their "never-say-quit" attitude has been an excellent example for all of us. It reminded us all that you can still win it all while winning the right way. This really is what the Northwestern experience is all about.

OTTO GRAHAM
Sarasota, Fla.
January 3, 1996

Chapter 1

Year of the Cats

Reflections of an alumnus on NU's phenomenal season

That Championship Season

By Michael Wilbon
The Sporting News

WASHINGTON, Dec. 11, 1995 — It could be a Disney movie now, except as we know, truth is always stranger than fiction. The Bad News Bears were never as pitiful as Northwestern football, the school that once lost to Chicago Dental and the Denver Athletic Club. How many universities have more famous alums from the drama school than the football team? It's the sorry, comically bad 113-year history of the Northwestern Wildcats that makes this the mostly ridiculously delicious college football story since *Rudy*.

We're talking about a school 47 years removed from a bowl game, a school that once lost an N.C.A.A.-record 34 consecutive games, a school that went from 1976 to 1985 without once winning back-to-back games, a school that hadn't had a winning record in 24 years and had averaged two victories per season since. And it's not like there was a logical progression from two victories to five to a berth in the Liberty Bowl to New Year's Day. From out of nowhere, with virtually no warning, some guy named Gary Barnett, who'd never been a Division I head coach, says he's going to take Northwestern to the Rose Bowl and DOES IT! From 2-9 to 3-7-1 to 10-1 and No. 3 in the polls and a trip to Pasadena. Sherry Lansing, a Northwestern alum and the C.E.O. and Chairman of Paramount Pictures, would have tossed such a script.

Geoff Shein, a fifth-year senior linebacker who arrived before Barnett and has a little more historical perspective and appreciation, says of this season, "I feel like I've just been rescued. It was like being stranded in the ocean or on a desert island for many, many years and the plane just came in."

Michigan tight end Jay Riemersma, whose Wolverines helped Northwestern go to the Rose Bowl by beating Ohio State, said, "I just wish I'd have put some money down on it, Northwestern 8-0 in the Big Ten. The odds would have been incredible." To be exact, the odds in September were 200-1 at Caesars against the Wildcats winning the Big Ten.

Yet, Barnett had come up with positive slogans: "Take the Purple to Pasadena" and "Expect Victory." And corny as it sounded, the slogans became mantras.

The 1995 Wildcats' Road to the Rose Bowl began with a 17-15 upset of Notre Dame. It was NU's biggest win in its 113-year history.

ROAD TO THE ROSE BOWL

That Championship Season

Senior quarterback Steve Schnur was the Wildcats' field general in their 1995 journey to the Rose Bowl.

Even after winter workouts months before the start of the season, players would chant, "Rose Bowl ... Rose Bowl ..."

And of course, absolutely nobody outside the program paid attention. I'm a Northwestern alum, Medill School of Journalism, 1980. Unlike the Johnny-come-latelys, I've worn NU hats and sweatshirts for years, and I keep up with the football and basketball teams fanatically. I remember clearly hearing from college and N.F.L. coaches that they thought there was something different about Barnett, that he could be the guy to turn things around. I'd heard similar things about Francis Peay (1986 through '91, 13-51-2), about Dennis Green (1981 through '85, 10-45). Some very good football coaches, including both of those men, have been beaten down trying to reverse field at the Big Ten's smallest school (7,400 undergraduates), the Big Ten's only private school, and the Big Ten's most academically demanding school (and I don't want to hear a word from Michigan, Purdue or anybody else). Ara Parseghian (1956 through '63, 36-35-1) and Alex Agase (1964 through '72, 32-58-1) were even worn down by the demands.

Losing wore out everybody. One of my closest friends, Bill Kornegay, was on the team from 1979 through '83. He was there for the infamous streak, the 34 consecutive losses that were then an N.C.A.A. record. "We always had 11 or 12 guys who could have played for any school in the country," Kornegay says, ticking off the names of teammates such as Chris Hinton, Steve Tasker, Curtis Duncan and John Kidd, who've gone on to enjoy long N.F.L. careers. "But the other Big Ten schools had 22 to 25 players who could play anywhere. I'd go home to (Flint) Michigan and my friends who played at U of M would say, 'Our practices are tougher than playing you guys.' Athletes are eternal optimists and they have short memories because you fall and you have to get back up. But we took a lot of grief. A lot. As far as the football, it wasn't the best of times."

But because the profile of the school is unique compared with the huge state schools in the Big Ten, losing wasn't merely accepted, it was something akin to a badge of honor. As my friend Ray Ratto wrote in The San Francisco Examiner, "It was as if the media guide cover once bore the legend, 'We're Smart, We Don't Have To Win' and that the attitude on campus was like, 'Oh, I'm sorry, we were busy producing Nobel Prize winners. Were we supposed to beat Purdue last Saturday, too?'"

Ratto nailed it. We'd leave the library on Saturday, go to dinner and ask, "How much did we lose by?" If the score was something like Ohio State, 35-17, I'd walk down the hall and ask one of the players how in the hell we got so close. Instead of throwing me out the door, somebody would patiently explain it, we'd both go back to the library and that was that. There was periodic talk that Northwestern should drop out of the Big Ten, or be kicked out, because it was simply impossible to achieve an Ivy League-level education while playing successful Big Ten football.

So it's against this backdrop that Barnett talked about taking a school that hadn't won a Big Ten championship outright since 1936 to the Rose Bowl. As he told The Washington Post's J.A. Adande, another fellow alum from the journalism school, "I opened my mouth at a basketball game one night and it came out. So I was stuck. There it was, I laid it out. I thought it was kind of catchy. It sounded good at the time."

Linebacker Pat Fitzgerald was the inspirational leader of NU's much improved defense.

It sounds absolutely fabulous now. No less than The Man himself, Michael Jordan, says Northwestern football is a bigger story in Chicago right now than the Bulls, which is true. Barnett, of course, is a genius. If history repeats itself and he goes to Notre Dame, like Parseghian did, we'll have mass suicides. Kids who never heard of Northwestern now want to go there, which turns recruiting into selecting. In much the same way the profile of already prestigious Georgetown University jumped when John Thompson's Hoyas became a power, Northwestern's profile has grown exponentially from Labor Day to Thanksgiving. There aren't enough recruiters to go around. I'm talking about people who recruit chemists, not linebackers.

The Monday after Michigan (now my second favorite school) beat Ohio State to put us in the Rose Bowl, the phone system on campus crashed under the weight of all of the calls from the tens of thousands of alums seeking tickets. When I called two friends from Southern Cal to ask them, if tickets are always this big a problem, they stopped yawning long enough to tell me it was no big deal, what with U.S.C. having been to the Rose Bowl 18 times before this. Northwestern, on the other hand, has 47 years worth of alums who've never been to any bowl, let alone the granddaddy of 'em all.

And these aren't just regular people we're dealing with here. Northwestern has to have more VIP alums than anybody, the kind of people who need tickets for their body guards and publicists and private photographers. You say Harvard does? I say, I don't think so. Here's a partial list, keeping in mind that alumnus doesn't mean "graduate;" it means the person attended the school. Some of our drama school people had some, shall we say, eligibility remaining when they left campus hardship for the bright lights:

Claude Akins, Warren Beatty, Richard Benjamin, Edgar Bergen, Karen Black, Kate Collins, Cindy Crawford, Patti Davis, Mary Frann, Tony Award winner Frank Galati, Brad Hall, Marg Helgenburger (the hooker on China Beach), Sherry Lansing, Cloris Leachman, Shelly Long, Julia Louis-Dreyfus, Paul Lynde, Garry Marshall, Ann-Margret, Patricia Neal, Paula Prentiss, Tony Randall, Daphne Maxwell Reid, David Schwimmer, McLean Stevenson, Peter Strauss and Charlton Heston from stage and screen. (I mean, we got Moses, for crying out loud. I don't understand how we lost all these years with Moses on our side.)

George McGovern, Dick Gephardt, Newton Minow, John Paul Stevens, Adlai Stevenson II, former Illinois Gov. James Thompson and former Chicago Mayor Harold Washington from government and politics.

Mike Adamle, tennis player Katrina Adams, Irv Cross, Eddie Einhorn, Otto Graham, Todd Martin, Billy McKinney, Brent Musburger, football player-turned-columnist Rick Telander, N.B.A. talent maven Rick Sund and Fred (The Hammer) Williamson. Yes, that Hammer.

Other than Saul Bellow, we won't get into all of the writers, most of whom, ironically, seem to write about sports.

You think ABC-TV won't love being able to pan those famous faces during the game? Let's face it, the Rose Bowl had become pretty stale of late, not to mention somewhat of a scrooge for not joining the Bowl Alliance in an attempt to produce something close to a national championship. This year the Rose Bowl has unthinkably been bailed out by Northwestern.

Sophomore Darnell Autry proved to be a gem for the Wildcats. He rushed for over 1,700 yards, earned all-America honors and finished fourth in the Heisman Trophy balloting.

Even a story this sweet hasn't been without a hint of controversy. With success comes scrutiny. Now it's being said that Northwestern must have let in some ringers, made exceptions, abandoned its lofty academic standards to recruit some kids who couldn't have qualified previously.

But the players who make up this year's team averaged nearly 1,100 on their S.A.T.'s and averaged 3.21 G.P.A.'s. The people who started this rumor about Northwestern lowering its standards obviously haven't paid attention to Duke basketball, or for that matter, to Stanford football. While we did sit in Dyche Stadium chanting, "S.A.T.'s, S.A.T.'s, S.A.T.'s" (usually at Minnesota). "SAFETY SCHOOL ... SAFETY SCHOOL ..." (usually at Illinois) and "That's Alright/That's OK/You're Gonna Work For Us Someday" (at everybody), scholarship and athletic excellence aren't mutually exclusive, as female student-athletes prove all the time.

Freshman Levelle Brown from suburban Chicago says, "One of the best things about this is proving all the people wrong who said NU could never be great unless it dropped its academic standards."

On-the-field accomplishments produced six All-Big Ten players: guard Ryan Padgett, center Rob Johnson, injured kicker Sam Valenzisi, injured linebacker Pat Fitzgerald, and Darnell Autry, who rushed for at least 100 yards in every game this season and a school-record 1,675 yards and 14 touchdowns. Autry, neatly enough, is a drama major. Four more Wildcats made the second team. Four more were honorable mentions.

Barnett may be brilliant but he also has talent, or at least cultivated it. "You don't see many jockeys carry horses across the finish line," he says in an attempt to spread praise to his players. NU was No. 1 in the nation in scoring defense (12.7 points per game), No. 3 nationally in turnover margin, No. 9 nationally in punt returns thanks to Brian Musso and No. 11 nationally in pass defense thanks to an out-of-this-world secondary that includes safeties William Bennett and Eric Collier and cornerbacks Rodney Ray, Chris Martin and Marcel Price.

The defense forced 16 fumbles and 16 interceptions, while the offense turned the ball over a school-record low 12 times. The best news is that nine of the

It took Gary Barnett 3 years to change the attitudes of NU players, fans and alumni. In year 4, he showed them how to be winners.

11 starters on offense come back next year, and the defense will get back eight players who have started all or some of the time. If this season is a fluke, then the same cast is going to have to crash and burn next season.

Despite all of this and a nine-game winning streak with victories at Notre Dame (the first since 1961), at Michigan (first since 1959), and over Penn State, the Wildcats are five-point underdogs to 8-2-1 Southern Cal, which had something of a disappointing season.

Barnett has been preaching all season that the team has earned more attention than respect. ESPN analyst and former Indiana coach Lee Corso has picked Northwestern to lose almost every week and has looked silly almost every week. Before the Michigan-Ohio State game, senior tackle Brian Kardos said, "We're just waiting for Lee Corso to pick Ohio State, then we know we're in the Rose Bowl." Corso didn't disappoint.

My friend Kornegay, now a manufacturing executive in the food business, looks at the team and sees some real differences from the ones he played on, starting with the physical conditioning that results in part from improved athletic facilities on campus. "The other big thing," he says, "is they're playing fourth- and fifth-year players along both lines and at quarterback, instead of freshmen." Kornegay rattled off the names of several freshmen who started at quarterback during his time. "The thing I like about Barnett when I went to one of those alumni games," he says, "was that he said he was going to 'grow a team.' It was as if he was taking the Japanese business approach, planning for the long haul instead of looking for quick fixes and short cuts to result in a quick profit. Not playing a bunch of young guys right away, even if they have more talent, is part of that plan. The only way I could be happier for these guys is if I was still playing myself."

Everybody wants to play again now. We all want to attend games, even though as students we all used to leave at halftime if we went at all. "From the time we shut down Notre Dame on fourth down in the fourth quarter of the opener, I knew we had arrived," Fitzgerald says.

It has been such a dizzying ride, we've forgotten about the Week 2 loss to Miami of Ohio, and with good reason. Even if Northwestern were 11-0, we'd still be ranked No. 3, behind Nebraska and Florida, and we'd still be headed for the Rose Bowl. And for a people who have never experienced what it's like to be excited about their team, their alma mater, in November and December and even January, this is the season in which not even fantasy could match reality.

Wildcat fans were treated to many thrilling moments by Brian Musso's daring punt returns.

CHAPTER 2

D'Wayne Bates (5) challenges Notre Dame's Brian McGee (17) en route to the Irish goal line.

Cats Shock Irish

Autry, Schnur Lead NU to Greatest Win Ever

BY CLIFTON BROWN
Special to The New York Times

SOUTH BEND, Ind., Sept. 2, 1995 — This was more than just an opening-game loss for the Fighting Irish. This was a shocker. Coming off a disappointing 6-3-1 record last season, Notre Dame began what was planned as a resurgent campaign this afternoon by losing at home, 17-15, to Northwestern, a team that was expected to be easy prey.

How stunning was this? Northwestern had not beaten Notre Dame since 1962, a 14-game losing streak. The Fighting Irish were ranked among the nation's top 10 teams in virtually every preseason poll and had the highest winning percentage of any Division I school (.760). Northwestern has not had a winning season since 1971, had the fourth-lowest winning percentage in Division I (.418) and set a Division I-A record by losing 34 games in a row from 1979 to 1982.

However, this afternoon belonged to Northwestern and its fourth-year head coach, Gary Barnett, who enjoyed the biggest victory of his career. While giving praise to Notre Dame, Barnett said he was confident of victory, and that the time had come to stop selling his school's program short.

"Our coaches did a great job of planning, and our players did a great job of executing," Barnett said. "We believed we were going to win. Before we left the hotel this morning, I told our players I did not want to be carried off the field. We were going to go over and act like we had done this before."

It was one of the most disappointing losses in the career of Lou Holtz, who remained one victory short of becoming the 15th college football coach to win 200 games. Holtz used to make winning games at Notre Dame look easy. But this performance will only put more pressure on a program that is expected to win not only this year, but every year.

"The players hurt, I hurt, we all hurt," a subdued Holtz said. "I am very disappointed. On offense, there was no real consistency. We were just out of sync, but I still have to give credit to Northwestern. They played a fine ball game."

Northwestern took a 17-9 lead into the fourth quarter, and Notre Dame's rally fell short. The Fighting Irish had a chance to tie the game with 6 minutes 16 seconds to play, after Randy Kinder scored on a 2-yard touchdown run to cap a 45-yard drive. But Notre Dame bungled the two-point conversion attempt that would have tied the game when quarterback Ron Powlus tripped over an offensive lineman's foot backing out of center. Powlus fell to the ground, killing the play.

"Derrick (Mayes) was wide open

NU-IRISH FACTS

- Northwestern was a 27-point underdog.
- NU had lost 14 games in a row to Notre Dame (last win in 1962).
- The Wildcats hadn't won an opener since 1975.
- It was Notre Dame's first loss in a season opener since 1986 when Michigan won, 24-23, in Lou Holtz's first game as Irish coach.
- Notre Dame entered with the highest winning percentage of any Division I school (.760), the most national championships (eight) and the most Heisman Trophy winners (seven). Northwestern had one of the lowest winning percentages (.418) and owns the Division 1-A record for the most consecutive losses, 34 from 1979-82.

Darnell Autry (24) sweeps left end for big yardage against the Irish defense. At the end of the afternoon, he would finish the contest with 160 yards on 33 carries.

Gary Barnett and his squad are left to wait momentarily before entering hallowed Notre Dame Stadium. Prior to departing from the locker room, Barnett gave his team only two instructions: 1) to "expect victory" and 2) to "not carry me off the field after we win. Act like you've done this before."

That Championship Season

Wildcats quarterback Steve Schnur (10) had a memorable afternoon against Notre Dame. He connected on 14 of 28 passes for two touchdowns in the 17-15 victory.

THAT CHAMPIONSHIP SEASON

Northwestern's stingy defense continually stopped the vaunted Irish at key plays. On one of the game's biggest plays, the Wildcats' defense halted the Irish on 4th down and 2 at the NU 44-yard line with 4:02 left in the contest.

ROAD TO THE ROSE BOWL

on that play, and I'm pretty sure we would've gotten the 2 points," said Powlus, who was 17 of 26 for 175 yards while being sacked four times and failing to throw a touchdown pass. "It's disappointing, but we still have 10 games to play. Things fell apart last year. I think this team will correct things and get back on track."

Notre Dame's final possession started with 5:12 to play, but after three plays the Fighting Irish faced fourth and 2 from their own 44-yard line with 4:02 left. Notre Dame went for a first down after a timeout, but the Wildcats stopped the play cold. Kinder took a handoff and tested the middle of Northwestern's defensive line. He was stopped in his tracks after a 1-yard gain by a group of Wildcats, led by Matt Rice.

"Maybe we should have punted," said Holtz, second-guessing himself. "We had two timeouts left. We could have held them and gotten the ball back. We probably should've punted. Hindsight is always 20-20."

Taking over on downs, Northwestern made two first downs and ran out the clock. The bench exploded in jubilation. The Wildcats entered this game looking for respect and a victory. They achieved both.

"We can't think of it as just another game," said Darnell Autry, Northwestern's tailback, who was the offensive star of the game with 160 yards on 33 carries. "It's Notre Dame. They have Touchdown Jesus, The Golden Dome. Playing here just isn't normal."

But today, Northwestern made itself at home. Steve Schnur, Northwestern's poised senior quarterback, completed 14 of 28 passes for 165 yards and two touchdowns, with no interceptions. Many of Schnur's completions came on key third-down plays.

Northwestern 17
Notre Dame 15

Northwestern	7	3	7	0-17
Notre Dame	0	9	0	6-15

NU: Beazley 7-yard pass from Schnur (Valenzisi kick)
ND: FG Kopka 35 yards
NU: FG Valenzisi 37 yards
ND: Farmer 5-yard run (kick failed)
NU: Bates 26-yard pass from Schnur (Valenzisi kick)
ND: Kinder 2-yard run (pass failed)
A: 59,075

	NU	ND
First downs	14	20
Rushes-yards	39-165	47-196
Passing	166	175
Return yards	67	-3
Comp-att-int	14-28-0	17-26-0
Punts	9-37	7-45
Fumbles-lost	1-1	2-2
Penalties-yards	7-54	1-6
Time of possession	28:17	31:43

RUSHING: Northwestern, D. Autry 33-160, A. Autry 1-5, Hartl 1-4, Schnur 4-(minus 4). Notre Dame, Farmer 16-85, Kinder 12-58, Edwards 10-49, Stokes 2-15, Mosley 1-3, Powlus 6-(minus 24).
PASSING: Northwestern, Schnur 14-28-0-165. Notre Dame, Powlus 17-26-0-175.
RECEIVING: Northwestern, Bates 4-58, Musso 2-42, Beazley 2-28, Hartl 2-25, D. Autry 2-8, Graham 1-3, Drexler 1-2. Notre Dame, Mayes 8-94, Edwards 4-37, Mosley 1-25, Chryplewicz 1-13, Farmer 1-6, Wallace 1-5, Kinder 1-(minus 6).

Northwestern never trailed, capitalizing on an early fumble by Kinder to drive 50 yards for a 7-0 lead. After the two teams traded field goals, Notre Dame pulled to within 10-9 on a 5-yard touchdown run by Robert Farmer with 2:35 left before halftime.

But Kevin Kopka missed the extra point wide right, which turned out to be a key miss.

After a lackluster first half, the Fighting Irish probably expected to take control early in the third quarter. Forget it. Notre Dame's opening second-half drive netted three plays and a punt.

Then Northwestern went for the jugular, driving 55 yards in just three plays to take a 17-9 lead. Autry busted off right tackle for a 29-yard run down to Notre Dame's 26-yard line.

With Notre Dame on the defensive, the Wildcats scored on the next play. Schnur spotted D'Wayne Bates streaking across the middle of the field on a crossing pattern. Schnur's pass led Bates perfectly, and he grabbed the ball at the 2-yard line, then dived in for the score.

The Notre Dame fans among the crowd of 59,075 were shocked. So were the Fighting Irish. And they never fully recovered.

This was no fluke victory caused by turnovers or gadget plays. Northwestern simply outplayed Notre Dame, as the Wildcats kept constant pressure on Powlus and Notre Dame's offense. Who would have imagined? Certainly not Holtz or any of Notre Dame's players. And with Texas, Ohio State, Washington and Southern California still remaining on their schedule, the Fighting Irish had a lot to think about.

That Championship Season

What Happened to the Parade and the Parties?

By Jim Litke
The Associated Press

EVANSTON, Ill., Sept. 4, 1995 — Just when the football team learned to walk the walk, the players returned home to find there was nobody to talk the talk to.

Let's face it: No one stepped forward to take credit for scheduling Notre Dame two weeks before Northwestern's students arrive because most years the trick is to have as few witnesses back on campus as possible.

And there was no reason to think this year would be different. Which explains why Patrolman Chuck Moran reported nothing even remotely out of place near Dyche Stadium, the home of the Wildcats and the logical place where the pub crawling should have begun in the waning moments of the Wildcats' 17-15 win over the Irish and lurched well into Saturday night.

No litter, no loiterers, no nothing.

"It was as quiet around here as any other Saturday night," Moran said, then shrugged, "Quieter, maybe."

Over at The Keg, a few blocks to the south, Cory Capps wrung out a dish towel, surveyed the thin Sunday afternoon crowd, then bit his lip. He tends bar to help cover the cost of his graduate studies in economics. Capps' pained expression made clear that in terms of profits, the weekend was already lost.

"I wish there were tales of wild drunken revelry from last night. Believe me, I could have used the tips. ... But the only screaming was some guy yelling, 'Go Wildcats!'

"And," Capps said, "I only heard him do it twice."

It could be the entire town, or at least those in the well-to-do suburb just north of Chicago who did step out, took their cue from Northwestern coach Gary Barnett.

While the team was preparing to make the trip from their Sound Bend hotel to Notre Dame Stadium, he called them together. "I told the players I did not want to be carried off the field," he recalled. "I wanted them to act like we've done this before."

Of course, the players could have been forgiven for thinking their coach had thrown a wrench. The last time anyone in a Northwestern jersey had beaten Notre Dame was 1962, when Ara Parseghian was coach of the Wildcats and long before any in the current crop of players were born.

That's not to say the idea of beating Notre Dame hadn't occurred to some of them. Linebacker Pat Fitzgerald, for instance, grew up in Chicago's south suburbs idolizing the Irish, but led the Wildcats defense with 11 tackles Saturday, then said without a trace of irony: "I enrolled at Northwestern so I could beat Notre Dame."

And it's also not to say that the moment, rare as it must seem for the time being, wasn't there to be seized.

"Coach Barnett told us before we left the hotel that if we didn't think we could win not to get on the bus," said running back Darnell Autry, who netted all but five of Northwestern's 165 yards rushing.

"Did we believe?" Autry repeated a question. "Well, we all left together."

In hindsight, this was not the complete miracle it

Against a heavy Irish rush, NU's Steve Schnur stood, poised in the the pocket, waiting for the right moment to throw.

Darnell Autry led Northwestern's ground attack, rushing for 160 of the Wildcats' 165 yards against Notre Dame.

seemed. The only two teams Notre Dame has beaten in its last eight games are Navy and Air Force. Northwestern, meanwhile, was 3-3-1 at midseason last year before reverting to form and getting thrashed the final four games. But most of the problems that invited those beatings — porous offensive and defensive fronts and questionable play on special teams — have been solved by Barnett's recruiting.

And the attitude adjustment he has been performing throughout his brief stay in Evanston seems to be taking hold.

So persuasive is Barnett at times that occasionally he falls under his own spell. That's why his conversation Sunday was peppered with the names of schools like Duke and Stanford, where athletic achievements on the scale of "Northwestern 17, Notre Dame 15" isn't a once-every-couple-of-decades trick, and the term student-athlete isn't an oxymoron. (And most student-athletes, in turn, know what an oxymoron is.)

But he promised that by Tuesday, when it is time to go back to work, perspective will have returned. Not long after that, bartender Capps noted, the students will have returned as well, perhaps with something to cheer about.

"Get back when we get a bowl berth," he said. "Then I'll have some crazy stories to tell you."

That Championship Season

NU Took Advantage of Irish Mistakes

BY JACK SAYLOR
Special to The Detroit Free Press

SOUTH BEND, Ind., Sept. 3, 1995 — A disgruntled Notre Dame fan was waxing sarcastic Saturday after Northwestern's 17-15 shocker: "If we catch a few breaks, we ought to go 6-5-1 again."

To many fans, the loss resembled an instant replay of 1994. "I think that would be right in a lot of respects," Irish coach Lou Holtz said. "The kicking game was pretty good, other than the missed PAT, which is like, 'Other than the assassination, how was the play, Mrs. Lincoln?'"

The familiar litany included:

• The Irish failed to tie the game with 6:15 left when quarterback Ron Powlus tripped over a teammate's foot on the two-point conversion attempt.

• Randy Kinder slipped on fourth-and-2 at the Irish 44 with about four minutes left, and the Wildcats killed the clock.

• Two damaging fumbles by Kinder and Robert Farmer.

• Four sacks of Powlus.

• A missed extra point.

• Short kickoffs by freshman Kevin Kopka.

• The defensive line failed to produce a pass rush, and was punished for 160 rushing yards by Darnell Autry.

• Despite the recent shortcomings of the Irish — they have been a .500 team (7-7-1) since beating Florida State in November 1993 and assuming the No. 1 ranking — Northwestern's win was hailed by some as the upset of the decade, perhaps the century.

But the Wildcats' coach, Gary Barnett, isn't buying the hype. "We expected to win this game from the start of fall camp," Barnett added. "Our players have visualized this for the last three years."

ROAD TO THE ROSE BOWL

NU's Danny Sutter (50) and Eric Collier (33) celebrate after recovering a first-quarter Irish fumble. This led to the Wildcats' first touchdown.

That Championship Season

(At left) After the game, NU linebacker Danny Sutter (50) celebrates the Wildcats' greatest win ever. A poised Gary Barnett (below) joins NBC-TV's John Dockery in the walk to midfield for a post-game visit with Notre Dame coach Lou Holtz.

Chapter 3

Dashed Dreams

Cats Blow 21-Point, Fourth-Quarter Lead in Defeat

THAT CHAMPIONSHIP SEASON

An unfriendly meeting: Miami quarterback Sam Ricketts (16) gets wrapped up by NU's Hudhaifa Ismaeli while attempting an end run.

By Rick Gano
The Associated Press

EVANSTON, Ill., Sept. 16, 1995 — Northwestern made its No. 25 ranking and opening victory over Notre Dame look like flukes, blowing a 21-point fourth-quarter lead Saturday and losing, 30-28, to Miami of Ohio on Chad Seitz's 20-yard field goal at the final gun.

The winning score was set up when punter Paul Burton couldn't gather in Larry Curry's low snap. The ball rolled 36 yards down to Northwestern's 1-yard line before Burton recovered with 43 seconds left.

Miami (2-1) took over and lost 2 yards on three plays before Seitz, who had missed two earlier attempts, made the 20-yarder. Fans who made the trip from Oxford, Ohio, poured onto the field to celebrate with the Redskins, as Northwestern players and coaches walked somberly off the field.

Coming off its stunning triumph at Notre Dame two weeks ago, Northwestern (1-1) was ranked for the first time since the final poll of 1971 — its last season with more than four wins.

Steve Schnur's touchdown passes of 27 and 36 yards to D'Wayne Bates and 12 yards to Darnell Autry put Northwestern up, 21-0. And Rodney Ray's scoring interception return on the second play of the second half gave the Wildcats a 28-7 lead.

But Northwestern then began playing like the "Mildcats" of old — blowing snaps and holds on field goal attempts, generating little offense and failing to contain Miami's attack.

Northwestern still led, 28-7, in the fourth quarter when Sam Ricketts — playing quarterback in place of Neil Dougherty, who hurt his foot late in the first half — rallied the Redskins to victory.

Ricketts, a redshirt sophomore who led Miami to two victories at the end of last season, capped a 55-yard drive with a 3-yard touchdown pass to Jay Hall with 11:14 to play to make it 28-14.

For three quarters, NU fans had a lot to cheer about. Then in the final period, a series of Wildcats' mistakes allowed Miami to wrestle away victory.

That Championship Season

Northwestern's forward wall of defense: (left to right) Casey Dailey (36), Joe Reiff (94), Matt Rice (95) and Mike Warren (68).

That Championship Season

After Northwestern failed to get a first down, Ricketts completed four passes to account for all 68 yards on the Redskins' next drive, which he finished with a 9-yard scoring pass to Jeremy Adkins as Miami pulled to 28-21.

The Redskins got the ball back with 5:38 to go and Ricketts threw passes of 32 yards to Adkins and 26 yards to Hall before Ty King scored on a 2-yard run with 2:22 left. But Northwestern stayed in front when Ricketts overthrew Eric Henderson on the 2-point conversion try.

Northwestern wasn't able to run down the clock, and then came the Wildcats' final failure, from punt formation.

There were earlier glimpses that things wouldn't go smoothly for Northwestern even though it seemed in control.

With 1:55 left in the first half, Burton had a punt blocked by Dee Osborne, who scooped up the ball and ran 10 yards for a touchdown. And Curry, who had to replace injured snapper Paul Janus, foiled two second-half field goal tries with low snaps.

Despite the win over Notre Dame, Chicago-area fans didn't catch Wildcat fever. The game only drew an announced crowd of 26,352 in 49,256-seat Dyche Stadium.

Miami (Ohio) 30
Northwestern 28

Miami (Ohio)	0	7	0	23-30
Northwestern	14	7	7	0-28

NU: Bates 27-yard pass from Schnur (Valenzisi kick)
NU: Autry 12-yard pass from Schnur (Valenzisi kick)
NU: Bates 36-yard pass from Schnur (Valenzisi kick)
Miami: Osborne 10-yard blocked punt return (Seitz kick)
NU: Ray 20-yard interception return (Valenzisi kick)
Miami: Hall 3-yard pass from Ricketts (Seitz kick)
Miami: Adkins 9-yard pass from Ricketts (Seitz kick)
Miami: King 2-yard run (pass failed)
Miami: FG Seitz 20
A - 26,352

	Mia	NU
First downs	14	20
Rushes-yards	35-113	51-142
Passing	249	187
Return yards	84	71
Comp-att-int	20-39-1	13-26-1
Punts	4-39	6-36
Fumbles-lost	2-0	0-0
Penalties-yards	6-40	4-32
Time of possession	28:06	31:54

RUSHING: Miami (Ohio), McCullough 17-45, King 8-37, Ricketts 9-26, Dougherty 1-5. Northwestern, D. Autry 35-152, A. Autry 7-32, Schnur 3-10, Leary 3-8, Bates 1-(minus 7), team 2-(minus 53).
PASSING: Miami (Ohio), Dougherty 7-13-0-59, Ricketts 13-26-1-190. Northwestern Schnur 13-26-1-187.
RECEIVING: Miami (Ohio), Hall 5-76, Washington 3-26, Henderson 3-17, Adkins 2-45, McCullough 2-5, King 1-28, Banks 1-25, Beverly 1-13. Northwestern, Bates 5-90, Hartl 2-39, D. Autry 2-29, Beazley 1-17, A. Autry 1-7, Waterman 1-7, Leary 1-(minus 20).

The NU defense quickly closes in on Miami's Ty King. King would later score Miami's fourth touchdown.

CHAPTER 4

High-Flying Cats
NU Bombs Air Force, 30-6

That Championship Season

By Rick Gano
The Associated Press

EVANSTON, Ill., Sept. 23, 1995 — Darnell Autry rushed for 190 yards — 53 more than Air Force, the nation's No. 3 rushing team entering the game — as Northwestern rebounded from a devastating loss to beat the Falcons, 30-6, Saturday.

Last week, Northwestern (2-1) blew a 21-point, fourth-quarter lead in losing to Miami of Ohio and fell out of the national rankings. But the Wildcats looked even better against Air Force (2-2) than they had in a season-opening upset at Notre Dame.

After Northwestern wrapped up its first victory at Dyche Stadium in 11 games over two years, fans rushed onto the field and tried — but failed — to tear down a set of goalposts.

It was the second straight loss for Air Force, which, like Northwestern, was ranked before losing last week.

Using their option attack, the Falcons came in averaging 377 rushing yards. But they managed only 137 against a Northwestern defense led by end Casey Dailey, linebacker Pat Fitzgerald and safety William Bennett.

Meanwhile, Autry was a workhorse for the Wildcats, carrying the ball 37 times and scoring two touchdowns. Autry, who also caught four passes for 51 yards, has rushed for 502 yards this season.

Instead of trying to sit on a halftime lead, as it did against Miami, Northwestern added to it against Air Force.

After Fitzgerald intercepted a third-quarter pass by Beau Morgan, the Wildcats went 62 yards in nine plays. Autry keyed the drive with a 37-yard gain on a screen pass and capped it with a 7-yard run on the first play of the fourth period to make it 23-6.

His team unable to move the ball, Air Force coach Fisher DeBerry replaced Morgan with quick, 164-pound quarterback Tom Brown. But Brown fumbled with 10:07 to play, ending an Air Force drive at the Wildcats' 20. Autry followed with a 46-yard run to set up a 5-yard scoring run by Adrian Autry, no relation to Darnell.

Northwestern led, 16-6, at halftime. Sam Valenzisi kicked field goals of 46, 26 and 35 yards and Darnell Autry outrushed the Falcons, 101-63 yards.

Jake Campbell, whose fumble last year against Northwestern cost Air Force the game, fumbled on the Falcons' second possession when hit by Dailey. Bennett recovered at the Air Force 20 and, five plays later, Autry scored on a 1-yard run for a 10-0 lead.

Air Force's only points came on field goals of 26 and 39 yards by Randy Roberts. The Wildcats hadn't kept an opponent out of the end zone since beating Princeton, 37-0, in 1986.

Historically on the losing end of lopsided scores, Northwestern scored its most decisive victory since beating Wake Forest by 27 points in 1991.

Northwestern 30
Air Force 6

Air Force	0	6	0	0-6
Northwestern	10	6	0	14-30

NU: FG Valenzisi 46 yards
NU: D. Autry 1-yard run (Valenzisi kick)
AFA: FG Roberts 26 yards
NU: FG Valenzisi 26 yards
NU: FG Valenzisi 35 yards
AFA: FG Roberts 39 yards
NU: D. Autry 7-yard run (Valenzisi kick)
NU: A. Autry 5-yard run (Valenzisi kick)
A: 26,037

	AFA	NU
First downs	17	22
Rushes-yards	39-137	49-249
Passing	134	219
Return yards	0	10
Comp-att-int	13-27-1	17-23-0
Punts	4-34	2-31
Penalties-yards	4-27	13-112
Time of possession	27:40	32:20

RUSHING: Air Force, Brown, 10-40, Morgan 10-29, Wilkerson 3-18, D. Johnson 2-17, Campbell 5-12. Northwestern, D. Autry 37-190, Leary 4-26, A. Autry 4-21.
PASSING: Air Force, Morgan 11-25-1-120, Brown 2-2-0-14. Northwestern: Schnur 16-22-0-206, Burton 1-1-0-13.
RECEIVING: Air Force, Campbell 3-35, Hendricks 3-33, Ranger 3-22. Northwestern, Bates 7-110, D. Autry 4-51, B. Musso 3-29, Beazley 2-16.

All-America linebacker Pat Fitzgerald sheds off an Air Force blocker as he pursues the quarterback.

After Gary Barnett was named NU's coach in 1991, his first recruit was lineman Justin Chabot of Oxford, Ohio.

The Original Believer

Gary Barnett's First NU Recruit Reflects on a Four-Year Journey

BY RICK GANO
The Associated Press

EVANSTON, Ill., Dec. 2, 1995 — His head is shaved now, his body toned from hours in the weight room. He barely resembles that smiling guy in the team press guide, so natty in his jacket and tie.

Bigger, stronger, with a different look. Justin Chabot has changed, just like the team which he plays for.

Northwestern's 6-foot-6, 285-pound senior tackle has been there since the transition started. Four years ago, he was coach Gary Barnett's first recruit.

Other than Northwestern, only West Virginia and the local school, Miami of Ohio, showed much interest in Chabot. So when Barnett came to his home in Oxford, Ohio, he listened intently to the talk from the new coach.

And he bought it.

Now, only one month away from playing in the Rose Bowl to cap the Wildcats' remarkable season, Chabot knows it was the best decision of his life.

"Coach had this confidence about himself," Chabot, a sociology major, said. "When he says something, you believe it and he believes it. You can tell he's not throwing you a line, he believes he can do things and when you have someone leading you who has confidence in himself, it gives you confidence in yourself as well."

"When I came to campus for my visit, he gave his 'Purple to Pasadena' speech at halftime of the basketball game and it gave me chills. Everyone cheered and was thinking: 'That was a great thought; wouldn't that be great?' But I knew Coach Barnett believed it. I could hear it in his voice and see it in his eyes. That made me believe it, and I wanted to be part of it."

Northwestern's amazing success this season, from doormat to Big Ten champions with 10 wins in 11 games, is the product of long hours of weight training and physical discipline from players finally talented enough to compete in the Big Ten. The season also

A battle of brawn: Chabot fending off a Wisconsin rusher.

has been the result of a mental turnaround as well.

The Wildcats developed a confidence, despite the school's long tradition of losing, that they could and would win. Just like their coach.

"If you are going to coach it, you got to live it," Barnett said. "Those things you believe your players should do and the things you say to your players are important. You have to live the same way. If you don't, they don't see how it works and they don't get the connection."

In the previous two years, the Wildcats played well for part of the season, then collapsed at the end. Not this year. With the exception of a stunning loss to Miami of Ohio in the second game, they were the better team every week.

And they knew it.

"We never envisioned losing any game this year; that was the beauty of the team," center Rob Johnson said. "The confidence showed through even when we got down in three of four games. Nobody freaked or panicked."

"We were down, 13-6, at Michigan, then we fumbled a kickoff return, and they had the ball at the 20,

Chabot (61) and his teammates share a moment of glory following a Northwestern touchdown.

and we were playing in the Big House," Chabot said. "A lot of teams might have folded.

"But I looked on the sidelines, and no one thought the game was over. Everybody thought we would come back and win. No one even had to say anything. I looked around, and it was 'OK, we have to get it done.'"

And the Wildcats did, rallying for a 19-13 victory. "I think that defined our season," Chabot said.

Chabot, who overcame off-season knee surgery, can reflect now on some of the first words he heard on that recruiting visit Barnett paid to him four years ago.

Chabot said Barnett told him: "We just have to get a bunch of guys who want to win, and if we get people with the right attitude, we will win."

"The first two or three years, we didn't," Chabot said. In Barnett's first three seasons, the Wildcats won a total of eight games. "But we became a closer team. We knew it was going to happen. We thought it would be last year, but it wasn't ... We kept believing, and it's happened now."

Chapter 5

NU Routs Hoosiers
Autry's & Cats' Streak Continues in 31-7 Win

That Championship Season

By Rick Gano
The Associated Press

EVANSTON, Ill., Sept. 30, 1995 — Darnell Autry gained 100 yards for a fifth straight game, Brian Musso set up a touchdown with an 86-yard punt return and Casey Dailey scored on a fumble return Saturday as Northwestern beat Indiana, 31-7.

Northwestern's victory in its Big Ten opener before a small crowd of 29,223 gives the Wildcats a 3-1 start for the first time since 1963.

Sophomore running back Alex Smith gained 136 yards on 23 carries for Indiana (2-2) but was carried off the field on a stretcher with 9:32 left after he was tackled and suffered broken ribs.

The game was delayed 10 minutes while Smith was attended to near midfield.

On the next play, Hudhaifa Ismaeli hit Indiana quarterback Chris Dittoe, forcing a fumble, and Dailey picked up the ball and ran 43 yards for a touchdown to make it 28-7. Sam Valenzisi's 32-yard field goal with 6:30 left, set up by Barry Gardner's interception, completed the scoring.

Autry, a punishing and elusive runner, entered the game as the nation's No. 2 rusher and on Saturday carried 28 times for 162 yards, just 5 yards below his average.

Late in the first half, he bounced off a tackler, switched directions and raced 42 yards for a touchdown, putting the Wildcats on top, 10-7, at the intermission break.

After Valenzisi's 34-yarder in the third quarter made it 13-7, Indiana couldn't move on its next possession.

Musso gathered in Alan Sutkowski's 55-yard punt at his 8 and broke down the right sideline before Sutkowski tackled him on the 6. It was the second-longest punt return in school history, behind a 93-yarder by Otto Graham in 1941.

Autry carried on the next play for the 6-yard touchdown and a 2-point conversion made it 21-7.

Dittoe's 2-yard run, capping an 80-yard drive, gave Indiana a 7-3 lead in the second quarter.

Valenzisi kicked a 40-yard field goal with a second left in the first quarter to give Northwestern an early lead, the score set up when Ismaeli intercepted Dittoe's pass. The first quarter also featured a wind-aided, 90-yard punt from Northwestern's Paul Burton with the ball rolling about 40 yards to the Hoosiers'. It tied Steve Toth's 61-year-old school record.

Smith broke off a 61-yard run three plays later, but Indiana couldn't score. Indiana lost tackle Chris Liweinski and defensive end Louis Pinnock in the second half with knee injuries.

Northwestern 31
Indiana 7

Indiana	0	7	0	0-7
Northwestern	3	7	11	10-31

NU: FG Valenzisi 40 yards
Ind: Dittoe 2-yard run (Manolopoulos kick)
NU: D. Autry 42-yard run (Valenzisi kick)
NU: FG Valenzisi 34 yards
NU: D. Autry 6-yard run (Beazley pass from Schnur)
NU: Dailey 43-yard fumble return (Valenzisi kick)
NU: FG Valenzisi 32 yards
A: 29,223

	Ind	NU
First downs	20	14
Rushes-yards	42-207	44-213
Passing	194	45
Return yards	17	124
Comp-att-int	19-37-2	7-14-0
Punts	6-42	5-56
Fumbles-lost	1-0	1-0
Penalties-yards	7-70	6-57
Time of possession	32:59	27:01

RUSHING: Indiana, Smith 23-136, Batts 8-27, Glover 2-15. Northwestern, D. Autry 28-162, A. Autry 6-21, Leary 4-15.
PASSING: Indiana, Dittoe 15-27-1-155, Greenie 4-10-1-39. Northwestern, Schnur 7-13-0-45, Handorf 0-1-0-0.
RECEIVING: Indiana, Stoner, 8-102, Carney, 3-28, Ward 1-17. Northwestern, Hartl 3-29.

Sam Valenzisi kicked field goals of 40, 34 and 32 yards in the Wildcats' 31-7 victory over Indiana.

That Championship Season

Brian Musso's 86-yard punt return was the second longest in school history, behind a 93-yarder by Otto Graham in 1941.

That Championship Season

Reaching for the Promised Land

Moses & Sinatra Team Up to Inspire Wildcats Miracle

By Rick Gano
The Associated Press

EVANSTON, Ill., Dec. 9, 1995 – Steve Musseau has survived three heart bypass operations and overcome cancer. Now he's battling diabetes.

Still, he is a testament to positive thinking, a man with a unique perspective on life.

"He knows a little bit about adversity," Northwestern football coach Gary Barnett says.

On New Year's Day, Musseau will be on the sidelines of the Rose Bowl in Pasadena, Calif., where a group of young men greatly influenced by his outlook and perspective will be playing the biggest football game of their lives.

The 73-year-old Musseau helped the Northwestern Wildcats visualize success. He made them believe they would win despite their long history of losing and he even taught them how to sing, leading a rendition of "High Hopes" that would become a weekly routine in this season of seasons.

"It was a plan to establish a belief system, a plan to help create dignity, a plan to eliminate demeaning, a plan of trust, a plan of patience and faith," says Musseau, a motivational speaker extraordinaire who has been working with the Wildcats the past three years.

Musseau has become a regular at the Wildcats preseason training camp in Kenosha, Wis., where the team goes for three-a-day drills. At one team meeting, Musseau donned a fake beard, long hair and robe, said he was Moses and told the surprised players they had been lost in the desert for 40 years and it was time to reach the promised land.

"And here we are," says Barnett as the Wildcats, capping one of the most unexpected success stories in college football, take a 10-1 record into the Rose Bowl

against No. 17 Southern California.

Musseau, a former college coach at the University of Idaho, had two sons play high school football under Barnett, whom he also regards as a son. So when Barnett asked him to help change the mental and spiritual makeup of one of the country's least successful programs, Musseau was more than willing.

"Whatever he asks me to do, I'll do it," Musseau said recently from his home in Marysville, Wash.

"Steve came to represent what we were about and what we wanted to do and we weren't afraid to do that," Barnett said.

"It's a risk-taking group. ... He initially tried to teach our kids how to think positively, how to visualize, how to treat each other."

When Musseau introduced Frank Sinatra's version of "High Hopes" to the players, most of whom are in their late teens or early 20's, he initially received some skepticism.

"They thought I was kind of kooky," Musseau remembers. "It proved to be a lot better than they thought. Finally they developed the idea they would sing it every Thursday. They just kind of elbowed one another and were giggling. But before camp was over the year, they were singing it jubilantly."

Northwestern's remarkable season, of course, can be traced to more than just a new attitude or ability to perform a sing along.

There have been long hours in the weight room and the recruitment of talented players. Linebacker Pat Fitzgerald made first-team all-America, and running back Darnell Autry and placekicker Sam Valenzisi were second-teamers.

Darnell Autry rumbled for 162 yards and 2 touchdowns on 28 carries against the Hoosiers.

But Musseau removed any negative thoughts produced by the past, even as preseason publications once again forecast the bottom of the Big Ten for the Wildcats. When Northwestern upset Notre Dame in the season opener, Musseau got one of the game balls.

"He teaches you how to think, how to think to get things done, especially in adverse situations we face here at Northwestern," center Rob Johnson said. "We had so many negative vibes coming at you from every direction.

"You've got to get everything out of your head and focus on what you can do and what you are doing as a whole. He focused on bringing our team together. He just teaches you how to think positively and eliminate all negative aspects."

Barnett says: "He's like a Gandhi to our players, and they just listen to him."

Now Musseau will stand on the sidelines in Pasadena with his team, hoping they take what he imparted and win one more game.

"After we had been with them two years they started seeing things." Musseau said. "Hey this stuff really does work. They had great belief, and they trusted. That was the main thing."

THAT CHAMPIONSHIP SEASON

Casey Dailey (36), William Bennett (20) and Barry Gardner (55) in pursuit of a Hoosier fumble. Dailey eventually scooped up the ball and ran 43 yards for a touchdown.

The Northwestern Plan

Mission Statement: Our mission is to take the student-athlete where he cannot take himself. We will foster an environment that teaches young men to:

1. Relentlessly pursue and win the Big Ten championship!

2. Appreciate and embrace cultural diversity.

3. Achieve an exemplary foundation of leadership and academic success.

Mission Statement: Our program is based on the values of family, successful attitudes and team chemistry.

Family. We believe in honesty, integrity, strength of character, care and confidence.

Attitude. We embrace a commitment to excellence, loyalty, selflessness, trust and humility.

Chemistry. We teach overcoming adversity, establishing priorities, goal setting and the value of diversity.

The Northwestern football family is where there is shared responsibilities, care and discipline and an absence of special privileges.

CHAPTER 6

The Miracle Worker

Northwestern's Gary Barnett

That Championship Season

By Rick Gano
The Associated Press

EVANSTON, Ill., Nov. 23, 1995 — At first glance, he reminds you of Robert Redford. A bit taller, perhaps. But the quiet confidence and swagger is definitely there.

And so is the believability.

His name is Gary Barnett and he isn't starring in this month's number-one box office hit. Nor is he a politician or corporate executive gracing the front covers of *Time* or *Newsweek* or with sound bites on the six o'clock news.

Instead, he is a college football coach who has authored the greatest miracle story in college football history.

It is one that would make Frank Merriwell proud.

For Gary Barnett and Northwestern University, this gridiron Cinderella tale began nearly four years ago when Barnett was hired away from Bill McCartney's staff at Colorado. Barnett was a proven winner, having served as an assistant to McCartney's offensive staff for eight seasons.

In Barnett's first year with McCartney, in 1984, Colorado won only one game and finished with a 1-10 record. Five seasons later, in 1989, the Buffaloes were crowned national champions after defeating Notre Dame, 10-9, in the Orange Bowl to cap off a thrilling 11-1-1 season. At the time, Colorado's rags-to-riches story was often referred to in terms such as "miraculous" and "magical."

A year later, Barnett was hired by Northwestern to take on college football's greatest challenge: rebuilding a team and a program that hadn't had a winning season in nearly two decades.

But Barnett didn't back away from the task that awaited him.

A few weeks after his arrival on the Evanston campus, Barnett was introduced to the Northwestern student body at halftime of a Wildcats basketball game. There, Barnett told an enthusiastic, but cynical crowd, that it was time for a change in the Northwestern football fortunes. Barnett, optimistic like all coaches tackling a new frontier, said his aim was to "Take the Purple to Pasadena."

Many Northwestern students and alums snickered, "Yeah, right, Gary, and Evanston's warm in January."

This was, after all, Northwestern, where athletics were a respite from the library, where losing was a way of life along Lake Michigan, where students tossed marshmallows into the band's tubas during lopsided football games.

There was an infamous 34-game losing streak in the 1980's, innumerable one-sided losses and an inability to recruit the top athletes.

Northwestern was the laughingstock of the Big Ten, the "Mildcats." Need a win? Just play Northwestern.

Others who came before Barnett had tried to retool the program and repair the psyche that so many losing seasons had damaged. And they had failed.

But Barnett didn't care. As an assistant at Colorado, he had helped the Buffaloes blossom into a power. He attacked his new job with a fervor, trumpeting "Expect Victory" as his slogan.

He pitched this approach to recruits: Come to Northwestern to help build a program from the bottom up.

"Barnett came in with the idea of 'expect victory' when I was a freshman, and I wasn't ready for it," said safety William Bennett, now a senior on the first team in Northwestern history to win 10 games in a season.

After the biggest win in his coaching career, NU's Gary Barnett savors a victory walk across the Notre Dame Stadium playing field.

"It took a couple of years. People didn't believe. We took it upon ourselves to perform and to prove to ourselves that we can play against anyone. It took those three years."

Now, with the school's second bowl bid secured, with a winning season for the first time since 1971, with a No. 4 national ranking, a 10-1 record, a Big Ten title for the first time since 1936, Northwestern's evolution has been amazing, if for nothing else, because of its suddenness.

After all, even with Barnett's new psychology, the Wildcats limped to an 8-24-1 record in his first three years.

"We're a big-time program with big-time athletes," Barnett said after a 23-8 victory over Purdue in the season finale that gave the Wildcats an 8-0 Big Ten mark.

"One thing through this season that he harped on is for this team to leave a mark here, lay down the framework for something that may carry on for years," said senior cornerback Chris Martin, one of the stars of a defense that is the nation's toughest to score against.

"So if I've done nothing else this year, I can walk away knowing we've laid down a firm foundation that will hopefully last for years."

That Championship Season

Gary Barnett and Notre Dame coach Lou Holtz visit prior to their 1992 contest at Notre Dame Stadium.

Winning the Big Ten — or maybe just sharing it with Ohio State — seemed implausible this season. But now the Wildcats have a remote chance to do something even more unbelievable.

Should the three teams above them in the poll lose, the Wildcats could conceivably capture a national championship if they also win their bowl game. And in a season in which they beat Notre Dame and Michigan on the road and Penn State at home, who's to say it won't happen?

Barnett, 49, was so confident Northwestern would win its opener against highly favored Notre Dame he instructed his players before the game not to carry him off the field once it ended. He simply didn't want them to create a stir as if they hadn't expected to win.

And now with a Big Ten trophy and the school's first bowl berth since 1949 ensured, Barnett has nearly delivered what he promised. If Ohio State loses or ties at Michigan Saturday, the Purple will indeed be on its way to Pasadena. If not, they'll still be warm for the holidays, playing in the Citrus Bowl in Orlando, Fla.

But not even Barnett expected this kind of success so soon.

"Eventually," he said. "I didn't think I'd have it necessarily for 1995. I had it penciled in but I didn't have it for 1995.

"You got to have the right things happen and we did. There were too many good things here, too many positives when we came here and looked at it to think it couldn't be done."

He found players who could make the grade in the classroom. He built a defense, centered around linebacker Pat Fitzgerald, that allowed an average of just over 12 points a game and forced 32 turnovers. And he found a punishing, durable and dependable running back named Darnell Autry, who has rushed for at least 100 yards in 12 straight games and put himself in the running for the Heisman Trophy.

Most of all, Barnett persuaded the Wildcats they could win, even after a potentially devastating 30-28 home loss to Miami of Ohio that followed the win at Notre Dame and produced the refrain: "Same old Northwestern."

The Wildcats haven't lost since.

"This group has set a standard for all of us coaches and players in this program to reach for and try to go beyond," Barnett said.

"Anything less will put you right back where we were before. It gives us a license to demand more."

With his Wildcats leading Notre Dame, 17-9, in the fourth quarter, Barnett observes intensely from the sidelines.

NU's Memorable 1995 Journey Began Last Spring

By Earl Gustkey
The Los Angeles Times

LOS ANGELES, Nov. 30, 1995 – Gary Barnett, the Northwestern football coach, came to Pasadena on Wednesday to discuss the season that catapulted the Wildcats into the Rose Bowl for the first time since 1949.

"We are living proof that history does indeed repeat itself," he said, explaining that the first signs of what would be a 10-1 season began last spring.

"After spring practice, I felt we'd put ourselves into a position to step up a level defensively, that we could now stop the run in the Big Ten," he said of a program that was 2-9 in 1993 and 3-7-1 last year.

"And I could see that we'd have a good overall defense and very good special teams. With those two things going for you, you have a chance against anybody. But to get to the Rose Bowl, you need luck and a lot of other things."

Barnett said another major factor was the ability of his players to perform at a high level in the suddenly supercharged football environment of Evanston, Ill., where Northwestern had had 23 consecutive losing teams.

It wasn't long ago that Wildcat rooters, seeing Iowa thrash their team, began chanting, "That's all right, that's OK, we will own your farms one day."

Then, this season, an amazing chant burst forth at Dyche Stadium, during a victory over Iowa: "Rose Bowl! Rose Bowl!"

Barnett said: "The atmosphere around our campus has been as electric as anything I've ever seen. Remember, this is a school where not long ago we'd be greeted at the airport by coaches' wives and players' girlfriends.

"After we beat Purdue (Nov. 18), 3,000 people were at the airport. I enjoyed our locker room after the Purdue game, the joy on my players' faces. It was the first time I kind of stepped back and watched them enjoy it all. I felt like a father, seeing his children do something they didn't think they could do."

Evanston is clearly a different place today. Purple and white flags decorate homes in the campus district. Vendors selling Wildcat garb are everywhere along Central Avenue on game days at 49,000-seat Dyche Stadium.

The first three home games drew less than 30,000. Then, after the team came home from beating Michigan and Minnesota, Northwestern finished to three sellouts.

And please, don't ask for Rose Bowl tickets.

"There's plenty of room left on our bandwagon," Barnett said, "but we don't have any more tickets."

And no, he wasn't surprised by the 31-23 Michigan victory over Ohio State that put his team in the Rose Bowl.

"I felt all along Michigan had a great chance to win, and my players felt the same way," he said.

"It was a win-win situation for us ... we were going to a major bowl, no matter what.

"Ohio State won all year with a very powerful offense. I felt if they got behind and had to catch up ... I didn't know if they knew how to do that. They faced that adversity against Michigan and they couldn't do it."

Referring to a 30-28 loss to Miami of Ohio the week after the Wildcats beat Notre Dame at South Bend, 17-15, Barnett recalled the pain.

"We were up, 28-7, after three quarters, then the players stood around and wondered where they'd be in the next ratings," Barnett said.

"But it was something they had to go through; we see it now as part of the maturing of this program. It traumatized everyone for three days, then the players and coaches had to let go of it.

"If we hadn't, it would have trapped us."

He was asked if Northwestern's 1995 story is one to inspire the sorriest of losers.

"Any program can do what we did – providing you do the right things and most importantly you're working for an administration that wants to win," Barnett said.

CHAPTER 7

Stopping a Giant
Cats Down U-M in the Big House, 19-13

57

That Championship Season

In a contest which was won on defense, NU's Tim Scharf (52) and Chris Martin (16) attempt to halt Michigan's Tim Biakabutka.

ROAD TO THE ROSE BOWL

By Harry Atkins
The Associated Press

ANN ARBOR, Mich., Oct. 7, 1995 — The drought is finally over for No. 25 Northwestern. The Wildcats are for real.

Northwestern, taking advantage of No. 7 Michigan's mistakes, rode the arm of Steve Schnur and the kicking of Sam Valenzisi to 19-13 victory Saturday, the Wildcats' first triumph over the Wolverines in 30 years and first at Ann Arbor since 1959.

"This win is huge for our program," said Schnur, who completed 11 of 23 passes for 126 yards and one touchdown. "We believe in ourselves more every win we get. We have a confidence about us."

The Wildcats (4-1, 2-0 in the Big Ten) opened the season with a 17-15 win at Notre Dame and haven't been slowed much since. Northwestern's only loss, to Miami of Ohio, was the result of a botched snap on a punt.

"We all learned our lesson from that," said Schnur, who flipped a 2-yard pass to fullback Matt Hartl in the fourth quarter for Northwestern's only touchdown on Saturday. "It's a shame it had to happen."

Michigan (5-1, 1-1 in the Big Ten) turned the ball over four times and had six penalties for 41 yards, several at critical points in the game.

"Turnovers are a part of the game," Michigan linebacker Jarrett Irons said. "As a defense, no matter where we're put on the field, we expect to stop the other team. And it's disappointing that we didn't stop them.

"We're real disappointed in the loss, but it's over with. We'll watch the film, and learn from our mistakes, but it's over with."

Northwestern linebacker Pat Fitzgerald was outstanding with 14 tackles, including two for losses, and played a key role in stopping Michigan's last-ditch drive — which ended in Brian Griese's second interception with 1:31 remaining.

"This is a special group of kids," Northwestern coach Gary Barnett said. "It was just a great team win. It's a heck of a way to get to 4-1, beating Michigan and Notre Dame, away. I dream about those things, but it's hard to pull those things off."

Barnett ranked this upset ahead of the Wildcats' shocker in South Bend.

"For me, personally, this is a bigger win, because I was tutored in Michigan heritage by Bill McCartney," said Barnett, who was an assistant at Colorado before getting the Northwestern job.

Valenzisi, who broke Ira Adler's school record with his 10th consecutive field goal, was good from 29, 28, 32 and 22 yards as the Wildcats fought back from a 13-6 deficit.

It is the best start for Northwestern since the 1963 team, coached by Ara Parseghian, opened 4-1. Northwestern hasn't played in the Rose Bowl since 1949, when the Wildcats defeated California, 20-14. But the Wildcats appear in the hunt for a trip to Pasadena now.

"We've been thinking about that all year," Schnur said. "You've got to take them one game at a time. That's one of our goals."

Tim Biakabutuka rushed for a career-high 205 yards on 34 carries for Michigan. Darnell Autry had 103 yards on 26 carries for Northwestern, his sixth straight 100-yard game.

Brian Griese, making his second start in place of injured Scott Driesbach, struggled against the Northwestern defense. Griese hit 14 of 34 for 96 yards with two interceptions. He scored Michigan's only TD on a 3-yard keeper.

"We have to give them credit," Griese said. "They

Northwestern 19
Michigan 13

Northwestern	0	6	3	10-19
Michigan	3	3	7	0-13

U-M: FG Hamilton 41 yards
U-M: FG Hamilton 21 yards
NU: FG Valenzisi 29 yards
NU: FG Valenzisi 28 yards
U-M: Griese 3-yard run (Hamilton kick)
NU: FG Valenzisi 32 yards
NU: Hartl 2-yard pass from Schnur (Valenzisi kick)
NU: FG Valenzisi 22 yards
A: 104,642

	NU	U-M
First downs	13	19
Rushes-yards	32-100	46-250
Passing-yards	210	96
Return yards	15	9
Comp-att-int	15-28-0	14-34-2
Punts	7-41	4-41
Fumbles-lost	2-1	4-2
Penalties-yards	5-35	6-41
Time of possession	26:22	33:38

RUSHING: Northwestern, Autry 26-103, Schnur 6-(minus 3). Michigan, Biakabutuka 34-205, Williams 8-37, Griese 4-8.
PASSING: Northwestern, Schnur 11-23-0-126, Hamdorf 3-4-0-58, Bates 1-1-0-26. Michigan, Griese 14-34-2-96.
RECEIVING: Northwestern, Autry 4-26, Waterman 3-48, Bates 2-60, Drexler 2-51, Hartl 2-14, Beazley 1-16, Graham 1-(minus 5). Michigan, Riemersma 5-33, Hayes 4-43, Toomer 2-8, Williams 1-6, Tuman 1-4, Biakabutuka 1-2.

That Championship Season

came with some blitzes and got some pressure on us, and that resulted in some turnovers. They didn't do anything that confused us. We just didn't get the job done."

Remy Hamilton kicked field goals of 41 and 21 yards for the Wolverines.

The loss spoiled Michigan's best start since 1986, when the Wolverines won their first nine games. Michigan next has its second idle week in a month. The Wolverines play at Indiana on Oct. 21.

Northwestern's defense hadn't given up any first-quarter points until Hamilton's 41-yarder just 5:28 into the game. But the Wildcats made Michigan settle for another field goal despite a first-and-goal at the 4, in the second quarter.

After Griese's touchdown gave Michigan a 13-6 lead, Northwestern's Dave Beazley fumbled the ensuing kickoff and the Wolverines recovered at the Wildcats' 23. Biakabutuka raced 23 yards into the end zone two plays later, but the touchdown was nullified by a holding penalty.

The drive came up empty when Hamilton missed a 37-yard field goal and the Wildcats — aided by more Michigan mistakes — took over the game.

"The biggest thing in the game was Michigan's turnovers," Schnur said. "We didn't turn the ball over and they did. We saw other teams turn the ball over against Michigan. We didn't, and they did. That was the biggest factor in the game."

PURPLE AND PROUD

First and last: The Wildcats have had only one trip to the Rose Bowl, in 1949, when they defeated California by 20-14.

Good names, poor records: Since that trip to the Rose Bowl in '49, only one of the seven head coaches ended his term with a winning record. Ara Parseghian was 36-35-1 from 1956 to 1963. Dennis Green, now the head coach of the Minnesota Vikings, had a record of 10-45 from 1982-85. Lou Saban made a stop in 1955, when he compiled an 0-8-1 record.

Remember 1971? That was the last time the Wildcats had a winning record. They were 7-4 under Coach Alex Agase.

Already better: Northwestern's record is 4-1. It hasn't had more than four victories in the same season in 24 years.

By Dirk Johnson, The New York Times

Pat Fitzgerald lunges to make an open-field tackle of Michigan tight end Jay Riermersma (16).

Stopping to Smell the Roses
A New Contender, Northwestern Dares to Achieve a Bigger Goal

By Dirk Johnson
Special to The New York Times

EVANSTON, Ill., Oct. 11, 1995 — For years, Big Ten teams have been stopping on this leafy campus along the Lake Michigan beachfront to kick sand in the faces of Northwestern football teams, sometimes mockingly called the "Mildcats."

After all, this is the school that once held the college football record for consecutive losses, 34, stretching from 1979 to 1982. Not so long ago, Wildcats linebacker Pat Fitzgerald recalled, a player might offer bravely before a game, "Hey, maybe we can keep it close."

Suddenly, however, there is talk of the Rose Bowl — with Northwestern in it. Its down-to-the-wire victory over Michigan last Saturday at Ann Arbor catapulted the team to the 14th spot in The Associated Press poll, and to fourth in The New York Times computer rankings.

"I don't think my feet touched the ground" after the gun sounded to end the Michigan game, said Northwestern kicker Sam Valenzisi, who has made all 11 of his field-goal attempts this season. "Nobody in the country, outside the guys in our locker room and our coaching staff, believed we could win."

Northwestern goes on the road Saturday against Minnesota, whose star running back, Chris Darkins, rushed for 294 yards, including an astonishing 141 yards in the third quarter, in a 39-38 victory over Purdue last Saturday.

Missing from the Northwestern schedule this year is unbeaten Ohio State, the favorite to win the Big Ten. After Minnesota, Northwestern faces Wisconsin and then intrastate rival Illinois.

The last time Northwestern went to the Rose Bowl was 1949, its only appearance in any bowl. It has been 36 years since the Wildcats beat both Notre Dame and Michigan in the same season, and

ROAD TO THE ROSE BOWL

NU's game against Michigan was much more physical than their earlier clash against Notre Dame. Wildcats coach Gary Barnett later called this his biggest win of the season.

That Championship Season

After snagging a Steve Schnur pass, D'Wayne Bates races towards the goal line with Michigan's Clarence Thompson in pursuit.

their last winning season came in 1971.

The only blemish on the Northwestern record came against Miami of Ohio, a 30-28 loss that resulted from a series of blunders by the Wildcats, who blew a 21-point lead. At the time, the loss seemed to sweep away the ecstasy of the triumph over Notre Dame and threatened to spoil the season.

"This is as low as it gets," coach Gary Barnett said afterward. "A lot of people climbed on our bandwagon after the Notre Dame game. Now they're going to slide right off."

Surely many did. But they have come right back after the victory over Michigan, if the flurry of purple Wildcats sweatshirts now seen around Chicago means anything. And stores here that sell Northwestern merchandise have been deluged with calls from across the nation.

As well as Northwestern played against Michigan, it still seemed toward the end that it would wind up with nothing more than a victory for morale. The Wolverines, trailing by six points, had taken possession of the ball on Northwestern's 33-yard line with two and a half minutes remaining in the game.

It was the sort of situation in which the favored team makes a last march to snatch victory from the valiant underdog. But that scenario did not anticipate a blitzing defense that overwhelmed Michigan's offense and quarterback Brian Griese.

Northwestern's quarterback, Steve Schnur, meanwhile, completed 11 of 23 passes for 126 yards. He has thrown just one interception all season. Sophomore Darnell Autry rushed for 103 yards, his sixth straight game with more than 100.

Fitzgerald, who is leading the Big Ten in tackles, with an average of 13.4 a game, said the biggest reason behind the remarkable transformation of Northwestern is Barnett. "He believes," said Fitzgerald.

Barnett, 49, a former assistant at the University of Colorado under Bill McCartney, said he has tried to instill in his players the idea that they can go down in history for turning around the Northwestern program, a chance for greater fame than simply continuing a winning tradition at powerhouses like Michigan or Notre Dame.

Tim Biakabutka, who would rush for 205 yards against NU, is hauled down by Wildcats linebacker Ray Robey.

That Championship Season

"He's taught us that it's one thing to jump on a moving train," said Rob Johnson, the 280-pound center. "It's another thing to jump in front of the train and turn it around."

Barnett has posted a 12-25-1 record in his four years at the school. In the victories over Michigan and Notre Dame, the coach said, there were no stirring Gipper speeches from the sideline. "I don't try to get involved in the game once its rolling," he said. "If you're going to become a good team, you must be intrinsically motivated. If the motivation is extrinsic, it ultimately won't do the job."

For decades, Northwestern backers have excused the school's poor record in sports because of its high academic standards.

But Barnett said there are plenty of top-rate players in the nation who are also good students. "You just have to be willing to go into every state and look for them," he said.

One of them was free safety William Bennett, a football star and senior class president at his high school in Tempe, Ariz., who had offers of academic scholarships from a number of universities.

Bennett, a pre-law student, said he chose Northwestern because it gave him the chance to get a top-rate education, and, as a Big Ten athlete, "play against some of the best teams in the nation."

Now, it seems, Northwestern is being counted among the best teams in the nation. In the game at Michigan, it was an interception by Bennett that sealed the victory.

"It was the greatest sound I've ever heard," Bennett said. "The sound of 105,000 people, all sitting so quietly."

A 30-YEAR WAIT

Northwestern improved its record to 12-45-2 against Michigan in a series that started in 1892. The Wildcats' previous victory over the Wolverines was in 1965. Since then, NU had lost 19 in a row and been outscored 500-135. The losses:

Year	Loss	H/A	Year	Loss	H/A
1992	40-7	H	1978	59-14	H
1991	59-14	A	1977	63-20	A
1988	52-7	H	1976	38-7	H
1987	29-6	A	1975	69-0	A
1984	31-0	A	1972	7-0	A
1983	35-0	A	1971	21-6	H
1982	49-14	H	1968	35-0	H
1981	38-0	A	1967	7-3	A
1980	17-10	A	1966	28-20	A
1979	49-7	A			

Michigan half back Chris Howard struggles for extra yardage against NU's Chris Martin (16).

With Chad Pugh (77) leading the interference, Darnell Autrey (24) follows upfield, looking for an opening.

That Championship Season

'Mildcats' No More — Northwestern has Arrived

By Rick Gano
The Associated Press

EVANSTON, Ill., Oct. 9, 1995 — For more than two decades, being a Northwestern football player meant staring at the sidewalk while walking around campus. Eye contact with fellow students brought apathy at best, derision at worst.

Being the Northwestern coach meant low job security and even lower job satisfaction. Every time things couldn't possibly get worse, they did. This week's 52-0 embarrassment simply blended into next week's 61-14 debacle.

Smug comments were outnumbered only by supposedly witty putdowns. North-WORST-ern. The Mildcats. Lovable losers. The laughingstock of college football. It got old, but it never ended.

Until now.

After road wins over Notre Dame and Michigan, the Wildcats are 4-1 and ranked 14th in the nation. And ridicule has turned into respect for a program that averaged only two victories in the 23 years since its last winning season.

"I've been here a long time — many, many losses. I've won almost as many games this year as I did my first four," fifth-year senior Rodney Ray said Monday, two days after the 19-13 win at Michigan.

"The attitude is great. Everybody has the same goals, everybody wants the same thing. In previous years, we had problems with this, problems with that, players knocking their coaches, things that were holding the team back.

"There were many times I thought I should have gone somewhere else. Now I just sit back, look at the team, and thank God I'm part of it. This is a year I'll never forget."

Around campus, around the Chicago metro area and around the nation, the word "Northwestern" suddenly means football excellence.

Against a heavy Michigan rush, NU quarterback Steve Schnur (10) goes airborne with a pass downfield to D'Wayne Bates.

"On campus this morning, kids came up to me, guys I've never seen, and said, 'Congratulations.' It's a good feeling," quarterback Steve Schnur said. "In years past, I don't think other teams took us too seriously. Maybe they didn't have to. If they don't now, it's to our advantage."

The architect of the turnaround is fourth-year coach Gary Barnett. With two more victories, he'll accomplish something Alex Agase, John Pont, Rick Venturi, Dennis Green and Francis Peay didn't in the previous 23 years — a winning season.

"When I walked in here this spring and met with the players for the first time ... I sensed it right away and I let them know that this was a special group. So it isn't a big surprise to me," Barnett said.

"I don't think we've ever wanted to look at ourselves as giant-killers.

Someone said to me the other day, 'You're playing with the big boys now.' I said, 'No, we are the big boys.' "

Schnur was part of Barnett's first recruiting class.

"You could look at him and tell he had a desire to win and he was going to get his players to do it," Schnur said. "We were his first class, and as soon as we came in, he was talking that this was going to be the team that was going to the Rose Bowl."

Barnett refuses to participate in such talk now. He saw what happened after the Wildcats got a little too pleased with their season-opening victory at Notre Dame — a home loss to Miami of Ohio — and doesn't want the same thing to happen with Minnesota next on the schedule.

"No. No. No. We don't talk about it," Barnett said. "It's like letting water into a crack in a rock; it can break that rock up. We're going to hermetically seal that break."

His players are buying the message; bowl talk is at a minimum.

"All of a sudden, we're in the Top 25," Ray said. "But just as quickly as we got there, if we lose the next game, we'll be out again. We won the Notre Dame game and everyone praised us, but as soon as we lost to Miami, it was, 'Oh, it's the same Northwestern.' "

But obviously, this isn't the same North-WORST-ern. The old Mildcats wouldn't have played within four touchdowns of either Notre Dame or Michigan, let alone beat them both.

"With just the one against Notre Dame, anybody can say, 'Anybody can upset anybody.' But I don't know about two," Barnett said. "It gives us a lot more credibility."

ROAD TO THE ROSE BOWL

Northwestern's win over Michigan in the Big House in Ann Arbor was their first since 1959.

Top 25 polls
(For the week of Oct. 8, 1995)

	The New York Times		Associated Press		USA Today/CNN	
1.	Florida	5-0-0	Florida State	5-0-0	Florida State	5-0-0
2.	Ohio State	5-0-0	Nebraska	5-0-0	Nebraska	5-0-0
3.	Colorado	5-1-0	Florida	5-0-0	Florida	5-0-0
4.	**Northwestern**	**4-1-0**	Ohio State	5-0-0	Ohio State	5-0-0
5.	Nebraska	5-0-0	Southern Cal	5-0-0	Southern Cal	5-0-0
6.	Iowa	4-0-0	Tennessee	5-1-0	Auburn	4-1-0
7.	Florida State	5-0-0	Auburn	4-1-0	Tennessee	5-1-0
8.	Kansas	5-0-0	Kansas State	5-0-0	Kansas State	5-0-0
9.	Michigan	5-1-0	Colorado	5-1-0	Kansas	5-0-0
10.	Tennessee	5-1-0	Kansas	5-0-0	Colorado	5-1-0
11.	Notre Dame	4-2-0	Michigan	5-1-0	Michigan	5-1-0
12.	Kansas State	5-0-0	Alabama	4-1-0	Oklahoma	4-1-0
13.	Southern Cal	5-0-0	Oklahoma	4-1-0	Texas	4-1-0
14.	Oregon	4-1-0	**Northwestern**	**4-1-0**	Alabama	4-1-0
15.	Stanford	4-0-1	Oregon	4-1-0	Oregon	4-1-0
16.	Auburn	4-1-0	Stanford	4-0-1	Virginia	5-2-0
17.	Wisconsin	2-1-1	Notre Dame	4-2-0	**Northwestern**	**4-1-0**
18.	North Carolina	3-2-0	Texas	4-1-0	Texas A&M	2-2-0
19.	Minnesota	3-1-0	Virginia	5-2-0	Stanford	4-0-1
20.	Alabama	4-1-0	Penn State	3-2-0	Penn State	3-2-0
21.	Syracuse	4-1-0	Wisconsin	2-1-1	Notre Dame	4-2-0
22.	Oklahoma	4-1-0	Texas A&M	2-2-0	Iowa	4-0-0
23.	Mississippi	3-2-0	Iowa	4-0-0	Baylor	3-1-0
24.	U.C.L.A.	3-2-0	Washington	3-2-0	Syracuse	4-1-0
25.	Virginia	5-2-0	Texas Tech	2-2-0	Wisconsin	2-1-1

Call it a lost weekend for Michigan fans

By Malcolm Moran
The New York Times

NEW YORK, Oct. 9, 1995 — The team was led down Central Street in Evanston, Ill., where the concept of a police escort for the Northwestern Wildcats was long ago dismissed as a foolish fantasy. But there were the Wildcats, coming home from their first victory at Michigan since 1959 to a crowd of more than 1,000 at Dyche Stadium, one of a number of results on a Saturday that was best viewed through the looking glass.

Just look: Northwestern, No. 4 in The New York Times' computer ranking with its unbeaten record in Big Ten play, is a bad punt snap against Miami of Ohio away from a perfect overall record. The Wildcats (4-1) have the unforeseen opportunity of looking down at Penn State, which very nearly ruined Ohio State's perfect season but instead was left without a Big Ten victory.

CHAPTER 8

The New Guys on the Block

After Cats' 5-1 Start Big Ten Foes Suddenly Take Notice

That Championship Season

Road to the Rose Bowl

Dave Beazley (86) stretches for a Steve Schnur pass in the Minnesota end zone. After this attempt fell incomplete, Sam Valenzisi kicked a field goal on the next play.

By Ron Lesko
The Associated Press

MINNEAPOLIS, Oct. 14, 1995 — Maybe No. 14 Northwestern isn't good enough to win the rest of its games. Maybe it isn't good enough to go to the Rose Bowl.

Then again, maybe it is.

Darnell Autry carried 28 times for 169 yards and three touchdowns, including a 73-yard run in the fourth quarter as the Wildcats rallied for a 27-17 victory over Minnesota.

The win guaranteed Northwestern (5-1, 3-0 in the Big Ten) its best season since the 1971 team went 7-4, and it gave the Wildcats their best start since the 1962 team opened 6-0.

"This is very special to me," said senior cornerback Chris Martin, who lost 24 games his first three seasons. "I've been here when we've been down, and to step up like this is a great feeling."

Northwestern, which trailed, 14-3, in the second quarter, also stayed in first place in the Big Ten, a half-game ahead of Ohio State and Iowa. The Wildcats don't play Ohio State this season, and their two toughest remaining games are at home, against Wisconsin next week and Penn State on Nov. 4.

The Wildcats, whose Rose Bowl championship after the 1948 season is the only bowl appearance in school history, need just one more win to qualify for a bowl game.

"We're not Ohio State and we're not some other teams, but we ain't bad," NU coach Gary Barnett said.

Minnesota (3-2, 1-1 in the Big Ten), which hasn't been to a bowl since 1986, came into the game believing it might be as improved as Northwestern this season, and it played like it early.

The Golden Gophers became the first team this season to score a first-quarter touchdown against Northwestern, and they also capitalized on a blocked punt to take a 14-3 lead. But the young Gophers quickly came apart, and the Wildcats were able to take advantage of the mistakes. Two fumbles led to 11 points, including Autry's first TD as Northwestern tied it, 14-14, at the half.

"We made stupid mental errors," said Minnesota's Cory Sauter, who completed 29 of 50 passes for 303

yards, all career highs. "That's what kills you."

The Wildcats, who entered the game ranked seventh in the nation in scoring defense by allowing 14.2 points a game, sacked Sauter six times and limited Chris Darkins to 75 rushing yards one week after he set a school record with 294 against Purdue.

"In the second half they got down and we knew they had to throw it," defensive tackle Matt Rice said. "We could just tee off."

Minnesota never threatened in the second half until Autry fumbled at his 34 with 10 minutes left. But Northwestern forced the Gophers to settle for Mike Chalberg's 47-yard field goal to make it 27-17. The Gophers also hurt themselves with nine penalties, while Northwestern committed just two. "We've got to eliminate those mistakes," Minnesota coach Jim Wacker said.

"We've got enough experience, but we played like a rookie team."

Minnesota twice was called for defensive holding on one series in the third quarter as Northwestern drove to the go-ahead touchdown, an 11-yard run by Autry that made it 21-14.

Autry scored his third TD on a nifty run, weaving his way through traffic before outrunning Rodney Heath for a 27-14 lead.

"I was trying to be as patient as I could," Autry said. "The front guys just took care of business, and I just followed them."

Northwestern outscored its opponents, 34-3, in the first quarter of its first five games. But after the first of Sam Valenzisi's two first-half field goals, the Gophers took a 7-3 lead when Sauter threw 4 yards to Paul Kratochvil, who made his first career touchdown catch.

On Northwestern's next possession, Sean McMenomy came untouched to block a punt, giving Minnesota the ball at the Wildcats' 12. Darkins made it 14-3 with a 6-yard run.

A fumbled punt by Heath led to Valenzisi's second field goal, and a Darkins fumble set up Autry's 18-yard touchdown run with 5:42 left in the second quarter. Steve Schnur's two-point conversion pass to D'Wayne Bates tied it at 14-14.

Schnur was knocked out briefly late in the second quarter, but returned to play the entire second half.

"We just keep scratching and clawing," Barnett said. "We may not be real pretty, but we're sort of alley cats."

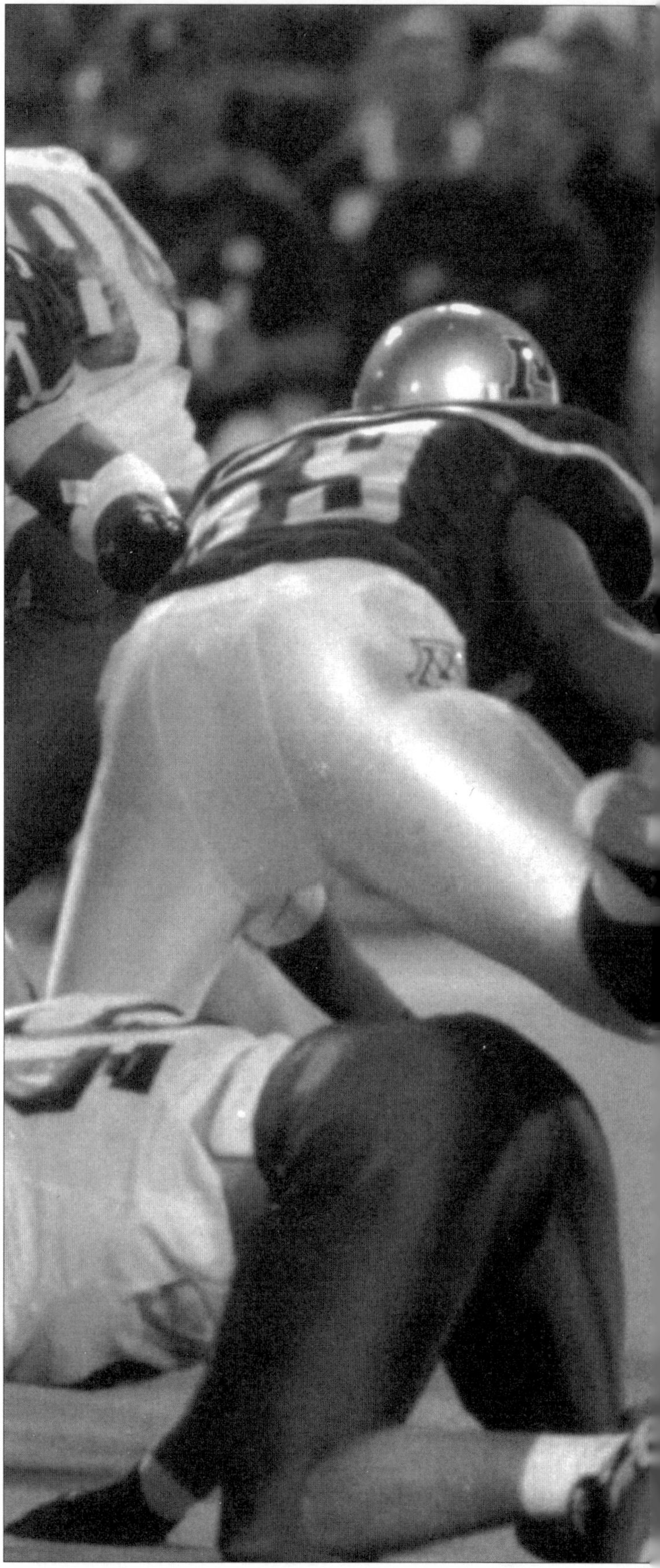

Northwestern 27
Minnesota 17

Northwestern	3	11	7	6-27
Minnesota	7	7	0	3-17

NU: FG Valenzisi 20 yards
Minn: Kratochvil 4 yard pass from Sauter (Chalberg kick)
NU: FG Valenzisi 29 yards
NU: D. Autry 18-yard run (Bates from Schnur)
NU: D. Autry 11-yard run (Valenzisi kick)
NU: D. Autry 73-yard run (kick failed)
Minn: FG Chalberg 47 yards
A: 50,504

	NU	Minn
First downs	17	23
Rushes-yards	35-192	33-51
Passing yards	200	303
Return yards	8	28
Comp-att-int	14-25-1	29-50-1
Punts	7-32	6-41
Fumbles-lost	1-1	3-2
Penalties-yards	2-19	9-70
Time of possession	24:10	35:50

RUSHING: Northwestern, D. Autry, 28-169, Hartl 4-17, A. Autry 2-6, Schnur 1-0. Minnesota, Darkins 25-75, Levine 1-11, Sauter 7-(minus 35).
PASSING: Northwestern, Schnur 13-23-0-194, Harmdorf 1-2-1-6. Minnesota, Sauter 29-50-1-303.
RECEIVING: Northwestern, Bates 6-100, Hartl 5-64, D. Autry 1-10, Drexler 1-18, Waterman 1-8. Minnesota, Theiwell 10-105, Darkins 5-55, Levine 4-22, Atwell 3-38, Woodson 2-46, Kratochvil 2-15, Reem 1-12, Tangen 1-7, Nelson 1-3.

Darnell Autry bursts through the Minnesota line en route to the first of his three touchdowns.

That Championship Season

A Record to be Forgotten
Twenty-three years of football futility.

Season	Coach	Big Ten Record	Overall Record	Season	Coach	Big Ten Record	Overall Record
1972	Alex Agase	1-8	2-9	1984	Dennis Green	2-7	2-9
1973	John Pont	4-4	4-7	1985	Dennis Green	1-7	3-8
1974	John Pont	2-6	3-8	1986	Francis Peay	2-6	4-7
1975	John Pont	1-7	1-10	1987	Francis Peay	2-6	2-8-1
1976	John Pont	1-8	1-10	1988	Francis Peay	2-5-1	2-8-1
1977	John Pont	0-8-1	0-10-1	1989	Francis Peay	0-8	0-11
1978	Rick Venturi	0-8-1	0-10-1	1990	Francis Peay	1-7	2-9
1979	Rick Venturi	0-9	1-10	1991	Francis Peay	2-6	3-8
1980	Rick Venturi	0-9	0-11	1992	Gary Barnett	3-5	3-8
1981	Dennis Green	0-9	0-11	1993	Gary Barnett	0-8	2-9
1982	Dennis Green	2-7	3-8	1994	Gary Barnett	2-6	3-7-1
1983	Dennis Green	2-7	2-9			**32-159-2**	**46-203-4**

Chapter 9

A Badger Bash
Wildcats Shut Down Wisconsin, 35-0

That Championship Season

By Rick Gano
The Associated Press

EVANSTON, Ill., Oct. 21, 1995 — These Cats are for real and they don't have to prove it to anyone. Not any more.

"I don't care what the country says. People thought we were Cinderella and sooner or later the glass slipper was going to come off," Wildcats coach Gary Barnett said Saturday after Northwestern routed Wisconsin, 35-0, to clinch the school's first winning season in 24 years.

"That didn't look like Cinderella out there today," he added. "If we play the way we did today, we're hard to beat. I think given the people we have beaten that we would have a chance to play heads up against anybody."

Even after victories at Notre Dame and Michigan, not everyone was convinced Northwestern could sustain such success. The Wildcats, ranked 11th, entered Saturday's game as 2-point underdogs to the Badgers, who were 24th.

But Wisconsin had seven turnovers and Northwestern, for one season at least, shed its loser's image and qualified for a bowl.

Thousands of purple-clad Northwestern students and fans, who've suffered for decades, mobbed the field after the final play in a homecoming celebration at a school known more for academics than athletic success.

"That's the most meaningful win from the standpoint we are assured of a winning season. That's what we came here to do," said Barnett, who has produced a winner in his fourth season.

"If they don't respect us now, I don't know what it's going to take for people to respect us," linebacker Pat Fitzgerald said.

"We're Northwestern. It wasn't like this before and now all of a sudden we win a few ball games. ... What has it been, 23 years since we had a winning season?"

Actually 24. But now no one will be counting.

On the downside was a knee injury suffered by kicker Sam Valenzisi, who Barnett said apparently got hurt while celebrating in the fourth quarter.

There was reason to be excited.

Northwestern (6-1) got its first shutout since 1986, ensured its first winning season since going 7-4 in 1971 and earned the minimum number of victories to go to a bowl, all on a damp, chilly afternoon.

The Wildcats don't want just any bowl, not with a 4-0 record in the Big Ten. They're aiming for Pasadena, where in 1949 the school made its only postseason appearance, beating California in the Rose Bowl.

"We're not thinking about what happened 40-something years ago. We're just thinking what has happened since we got here," defensive tackle Matt Rice said.

"We have stepping stones we want to get to. The ultimate goal is the Rose Bowl."

The Badgers, meanwhile, just couldn't get going, even though about half of the sellout crowd of 49,256, the first at Dyche Stadium in 12 years, was rooting for Wisconsin.

The Badgers (2-3-1, 1-2 in the Big Ten) lost five fumbles — they'd lost only one all season entering the game — and quarterback Darrell Bevell threw two interceptions as Wisconsin suffered its first shutout since 1989.

Northwestern sophomore tailback Darnell Autry gained 81 yards on 26 carries, ending his seven-game stretch of 100-yard games, but he scored two second-half touchdowns after Badgers' turnovers as the Wildcats put the victory away. They led, 13-0, at the half after four Wisconsin mistakes.

Wisconsin's Carl McCullough fumbled for the second time, this one after a pass reception on the first

---

Northwestern 35
Wisconsin 0

Wisconsin	0	0	0	0-0
Northwestern	10	3	6	16-35

NU: Schnur 1-yard run (Valenzisi kick)
NU: FG Valenzisi 32 yards
NU: FG Valenzisi 26 yards
NU: D. Autry 32-yard pass from Schnur (pass failed)
NU: D. Autry 3-yard run (Valenzisi kick)
NU: FG Gowins 42 yards
NU: Brown 38-yard run (kick failed)
A: 49,256

	Wis	NU
First downs	20	12
Rushes-yards	40-101	44-189
Passing	220	111
Return yards	12	78
Comp-att-int	18-30-2	9-17-1
Punts	5-37	5-45
Fumbles-lost	5-5	0-0
Penalties-yards	3-25	5-29
Time of possession	30:48	29:12

RUSHING: Wisconsin, McCullough 23-74, Roberson 6-29, Martin 5-9, Samuel 2-8, Torian 1-2, Stecker 1-(minus 2), Bevell 2-(minus 19). Northwestern, D. Autry 26-81, Brown 2-54, Schnur 7-32, A. Autry 6-13, Leary 3-9.
PASSING: Wisconsin, Bevell 15-23-2-193, Samuel 3-7-0-27. Northwestern, Schnur 9-17-1-111.
RECEIVING: Wisconsin, Simmons 4-72, London 4-49, Martin 3-24, Torian 3-36, McCullough 3-27, Sondrup 1-12. Northwestern, Bates 3-32, Hartl 3-21, Musso 2-26, D. Autry 1-32.

The Wildcats' crafty punt returner, Brian Musso (22), gathers in a Wisconsin kick before beginning his journey upfield.

scrimmage play of the second half. Three plays later, Autry caught a pass in the flats from Steve Schnur and went 32 yards for a touchdown.

"We made a lot of mental errors. This is a different Northwestern team. They are very physical, strong and quick," McCullough said.

In the fourth quarter, defensive end Mike Warren picked off Bevell's pass and returned it 53 yards to set up Autry's 3-yard scoring run as the Wildcats went up, 26-0. Freshman Levelle Brown's 38-yard run capped the scoring.

Valenzisi's 26-yard field goal with 56 seconds to go in the second quarter put the Wildcats ahead, 13-0, at the half.

Wisconsin freshman Aaron Stecker fumbled a punt and a kickoff in the first quarter and Bevell threw an interception, helping Northwestern jump to a 10-0 lead.

"I dropped it and I felt like I let the team down," Stecker said.

The Badgers drove to a first down at the Northwestern 12 in the second quarter, but McCullough fumbled after a 7-yard gain and the Wildcats' Chris Martin recovered at the 1.

"I thought I was down. But we focus on ball containment and I don't want to look at that as an excuse," McCullough said.

Stecker fumbled the game's first punt and Shane Graham recovered at the Wisconsin 27. Nine plays later, Schnur sneaked in from the 1 on fourth down to put the Wildcats ahead.

"Things started with that punt and pretty much snowballed from there," Badgers coach Barry Alvarez said.

Stecker fumbled the ensuing kickoff and Josh Barnes recovered but the Wildcats didn't score when Valenzisi, who had made 13 straight field goals, missed a 29-yarder.

Wisconsin's first scrimmage play of the game didn't come until 5:21 remained in the first quarter, and on third down Martin intercepted Bevell's pass.

Wisconsin stopped the Wildcats again and this time Valenzisi hit from 32 yards for a 10-0 lead.

"It's tough, obviously," Bevell said. "We didn't get the ball until there were about five minutes left in the quarter and we're not used to that. We just didn't respond after the turnovers."

It was another magical day for Darnell Autry, who scored a pair of touchdowns for the Wildcats.

ROAD TO THE ROSE BOWL

That Championship Season

ROAD TO THE ROSE BOWL

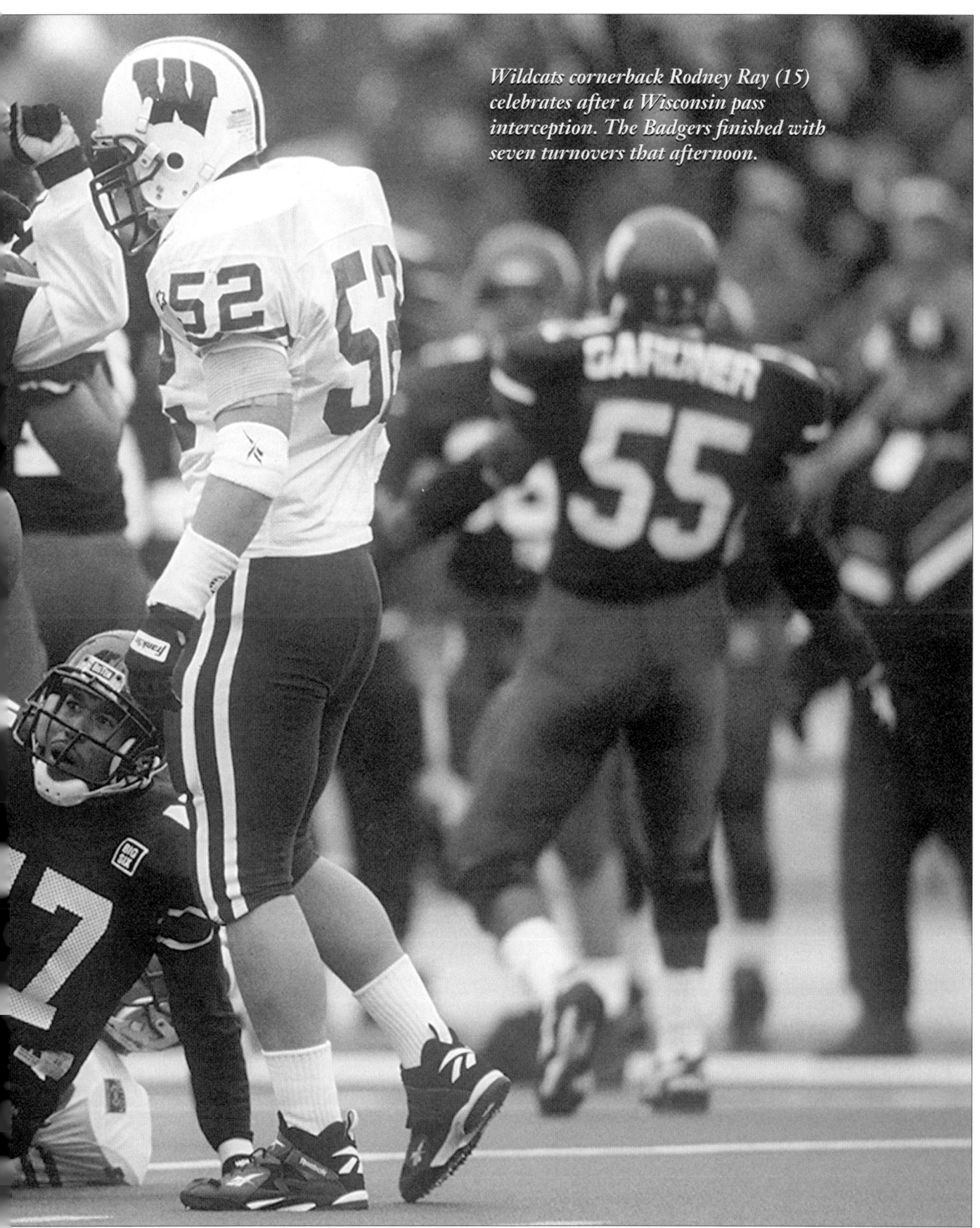

Wildcats cornerback Rodney Ray (15) celebrates after a Wisconsin pass interception. The Badgers finished with seven turnovers that afternoon.

That Championship Season

The Evanston Miracle

An Academic Heavyweight Enjoys a Rebirth on the Gridiron

By Malcolm Moran
Special to The New York Times

EVANSTON, Ill., Nov. 26, 1995 – Fred Hemke thought he had seen just about everything in his 15 years as the faculty representative to the Athletic Department at Northwestern University and more than three decades on the campus. He arrived in the early 1960's when Ara Parseghian was the football coach and Northwestern reached the Top 10 in a brief flirtation with success. He saw the school's purple flag flying at the Rose Bowl on New Year's Day, and assumed the Wildcats would never come closer than that. He watched athletes endure the humiliation of the 34-game losing streak from 1979-1982, and sat in on meetings when Northwestern's worthiness as a Big Ten member became the subject of an intense debate.

Now, at least, he has a response to that debate. "I've come to the point where I agree," Hemke said solemnly this afternoon and paused for the proper effect.

"I think we're too good for them."

And Hemke laughed long and hard, near the end of Northwestern's giddiest weekend, as the campus community, its longtime followers and an increasingly crowded bandwagon began to prepare for a once-unthinkable trip to the Rose Bowl. The second trip to a bowl game in Northwestern history – and the first since its victory over California in Pasadena at the end of the 1948 season – became that much richer because of the belief that the Wildcats had achieved their Big Ten championship on their own terms.

The notion that had existed for years, that an academically competitive university with an enrollment of 7,400 had no business continuing to challenge the largest state institutions in the Midwest on football fields, has been replaced by a run on roses and a scramble for tickets and souvenirs.

"It remedies, at least in my mind, a great amount of cynicism I have heard concerning intercollegiate athletics, particularly football," Hemke said. "That you can't maintain high academic principles and still come out on top. It is possible to do both. That is the greatest satisfaction."

Sam Valenzisi, a senior kicker, said the challenge to balance the athletic and academic demands is no more difficult now than it was when the Wildcats were losing.

"It's the same amount of time," he said. "It's not any different, except we're winning."

Valenzisi, who is working toward a master's degree in journalism, has been named a finalist for the Lou Groza Award for the outstanding place-kicker in the nation. And that in itself is startling on a campus where, for generations of students, the attitude toward football has been a mixture of stubborn loyalty, sarcastic humor and complete obliviousness.

"Many Northwestern students don't know football," said Sam Maniar, a senior psychology major from Cleveland. "At the games, you'll hear, 'Go for it,' on third down."

Normally, you go for it on fourth down. And normally, Northwestern doesn't beat teams like Notre Dame and Michigan, go undefeated in conference play and finish with a 10-1 record. But they did this season, and the crowds of 30,000 at Dyche Stadium at the three home games in September grew to the capacity of 49,256 during the final stretch of the believe-it-or-not campaign.

This past Saturday, when Ohio State fell to Michigan and Northwestern incredibly found itself going to the Rose Bowl, there was no dancing in the streets of Evanston, mostly because many students were away because of the Thanksgiving weekend.

But for those who stuck around, it became a memorable afternoon.

"I didn't know any of the people in the TV lounge, and we were all laughing together," said Elizabeth Pensgard, a junior English major from California, Mo. "Northwestern has had a reputation for being apathetic for social things, but this has been a great experience."

She was speaking in The Keg, a tavern in down-

Against Wisconsin, linebacker Casey Dailey (36) and the NU defense kept the Badgers' running lanes shut down.

town Evanston about a mile from campus. Danielle Lodewyck, a pre-med sophomore from Turlock, Calif., was nearby, talking about the four-hour trip she would be taking with her father, a Northwestern alumnus, from her home to Pasadena.

"When I first came here," she remembered, "people back home would say, 'Northwestern – isn't that a bank?'"

Now it's one of the top-rated teams in the country – No. 3 in The Associated Press poll and No. 5 in The New York Times computer ranking.

The change began when Gary Barnett arrived as the new head coach after the end of the 1991 season. He took on the painful memories and the bad jokes with an aggressive approach. His program would be captured by two words – "Expect Victory" – that would begin to appear all over town. He spoke to students at a basketball game in January 1992, announcing over the public address system that he planned on "taking the Purple to Pasadena."

Barnett had been on the job for a month. Now that his outrageous pronouncement has become reality, the coach admits he had no idea of how serious the deficiencies were. Years before, according to one source outside the university, informal discussions between Northwestern and Ivy League officials explored the idea of the Wildcats leaving the Big Ten to compete on a more modest level. The discussions were ended because of financial and logistical issues that could not be resolved.

So here was a coach, in a gym full of students, talking about going where?

"I was very naive and ignorant, really," Barnett said this afternoon as he sat in an office near the stadium. "I knew there was a longtime losing record. I didn't know the depth of it, and I didn't really know why. When I walked in here, I thought I was taking over any other program, and if I did this and this, shoot, we'd end up in Pasadena, eventually, if we set our sights high enough and kept working on it.

"After going through a season," the coach said, "then all of a sudden I realized just how far we had to go. If you asked me at that point, would I walk into a crowded basketball arena and say, 'We're taking the Purple to Pasadena,' I wouldn't have said it."

Barnett began to search for players he called risk takers. He consistently emphasized the need for the team to insulate itself from the negative discussions on the outside. However, Hemke said today, there were no concessions when it came to admission requirements. "Nothing has changed," he said. "And I'm as close to that as anyone around here. Nothing has changed at all."

Nothing has changed, and everything has changed. Valenzisi, the aspiring journalist, is scheduled to make his second appearance this week on "The Sports Writers on T.V.," the weekly round-table discussion among Chicago-area sports journalists who are old enough to be his parents and grandparents.

He will be at the Rose Bowl, with the other disbelieving players and fans, but he won't get to play in the game against Southern California because his season was ended when he jumped up to celebrate a teammate's tackle on a kickoff and tore a ligament in his left knee.

That's the old kind of Northwestern misfortune, the kind that's now overwhelmed by the new-found joy.

"It's funny when you drive around Evanston," Valensizi said. "Everywhere you go you see Northwestern banners and flags, people wearing Northwestern sweatshirts. But a lot of them aren't brand new. A lot of them, you can tell, have been in dresser drawers or stowed away in closets or foot lockers for 20 or 30 years.

"People have been waiting a long time for this. That makes me feel really good."

It's 47 years since 1949, or as Valensizi said, "47 football teams that have had the same dream that we had, that we're getting to act on right now."

"They are just as much a part of this as we are," he said with pride.

CHAPTER 10

Valiant Comeback

Trailing, 14-0, Cats Rally to Defeat Illini, 17-14

That Championship Season

By Rick Gano
The Associated Press

CHAMPAIGN, Ill., Oct. 28, 1995 — Pack the suntan oil and the short-sleeved shirts. Maybe the bathing suits, too. Northwestern's Wildcats won't be home for the holidays.

Officially, they still have to wait. But unofficially, after overcoming a two-touchdown deficit and a wild finish to beat Illinois, 17-14, Saturday, the No. 8 Wildcats are all but in a bowl game.

And they know it.

"Tell them we're going somewhere warm for Christmas. I don't have a guarantee but we've got pretty good percentages," NU coach Gary Barnett said after his team's fourth road win and seventh victory overall.

"I think we've pretty much locked ourselves into a bowl game and now it's up to us which one we go to," said Darnell Autry, who gained 100 yards for the ninth straight game and scored the winning touchdown on a 1-yard run with just over six minutes left.

Northwestern (7-1) rallied from a 14-0 deficit to stay atop the Big Ten with a 5-0 mark. The Wildcats' only bowl appearance came in the 1949 Rose Bowl, a 20-14 victory over California.

Illinois (3-4, 1-3 in Big Ten) moved into position to win or at least tie in the closing minutes before Eric Collier intercepted a desperation pass by Scott Weaver in the end zone with seven seconds remaining.

"We could have let this one slip away," Barnett said.

Weaver's 37-yard pass to Jason Dulick on fourth down gave Illinois a first down at the Northwestern 18 with 1:07 left. But the Illini, looking confused, let the clock get away.

They ran a play for a yard and then Matt Rice sacked Weaver for a 13-yard loss on second down, knocking the clock down to 26 seconds.

After a timeout for each team, Weaver fumbled the snap and was sacked again but Illinois was also called for holding on the play.

The Wildcats took the penalty and, on third and 37 from the 45, Weaver rolled out and heaved the ball into the end zone where Collier jumped up to pick it off.

"When Dulick caught the ball we were ahead of schedule and then it disintegrated on us," Illinois coach Lou Tepper said. "We didn't handle the at-the-line calls, we had a holding penalty, we had a sack. We didn't give ourselves a chance to win."

Barnett said, "We felt like if we put pressure on Weaver we could sack him. We had to do that because they were in field goal range. The last penalty we wanted to take to push them back as far as we could."

Autry carried 41 times for 151 yards, including 10 carries for 37 yards on the game-winning 58-yard drive that also featured a 19-yard pass from Steve Schnur to D'Wayne Bates.

A 4-yard gain by Autry and a face-mask penalty gave Northwestern a first down at the Illinois 3. Autry carried twice more, putting the ball on the 1-foot line before Schnur's third-down sneak was stopped short. After a timeout, Autry took a pitch left into the end zone.

"They had too many folks around in the center of the line. We talked about it and decided to go with the pitch," Schnur said.

"I wanted the ball, obviously," Autry said. "I know that if they need something and they call my number, I'm going to get something done."

A deflected pass that went for a 38-yard gain

Northwestern 17
Illinois 14

Northwestern	0	10	0	7-17
Illinois	7	7	0	0-14

IL: Weaver 1-yard run (Scheuplin kick)
IL: Holcombe 7-yard run (Scheuplin kick)
NU: FG Gowins 49 yards
NU: Bates 34-yard pass from Schnur (Gowins kick)
NU: D. Autry 1-yard run (Gowins kick)
A: 65,425

	NU	IL
First downs	16	15
Rushes-yards	45-153	43-107
Passing	117	198
Return yards	33	2
Comp-att-int	8-19-0	18-32-3
Punts	7-29	6-41
Fumbles-lost	2-0	0-0
Penalties-yards	1-15	9-77
Time of possession	28:06	31:54

RUSHING: Northwestern, D. Autry 41-151, Bates 1-3, Schnur 3-(minus 1). Illinois, Holcombe 27-100, Douthard 12-24, Weaver 4-(Minus 17).
PASSING: Northwestern, Schnur 8-19-0-117. Illinois, Weaver 18-32-3-198.
RECEIVING: Northwestern, Musso 3-38, Bates 3-74, D. Autry 2-5. Illinois, Dulic 8-93, Douthard 6-40, Cushing 2-23, Majoy 1-38, Holcombe 1-4.

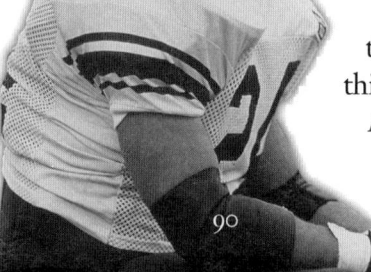

Always in a hurry to get to the quarterback, defensive lineman Matt Rice (95) charges past an Illini blocker.

and a 97-yard drive helped the Illini build a 14-0 lead.

Weaver's pass went off Dulick's hands as he was being hit by William Bennett, the ball went high in the air and Illinois' Rob Majoy caught it and carried to the Northwestern 8. On fourth and 1 after Northwestern had stopped two running plays, Weaver faked and carried around right end for the touchdown.

The Illini were pinned deep after a punt was downed on the 3. But Weaver converted two third-down passes, one to Dulick for 9 yards and the other to Matt Cushing for 16, as the Illini moved 97 yards in 16 plays. They held onto the ball for 6 minutes 33 seconds, scoring on Robert Holcombe's 7-yard run with 10:42 left in the half.

Northwestern's Brian Gowins, kicking because Sam Valenzisi tore a knee ligament last week, hit a 49-yard field goal with a 25 mph wind at his back to make it 14-3.

Schnur then hit Bates on a 34-yard touchdown with 4:40 left in the half, capping a quick 73-yard drive.

Collier stopped a late Illinois drive with his interception, leaving it 14-10 at halftime.

Acclaimed for his roving, hard-hitting play, Pat Fitzgerald (51) won the 1995 Chuck Bednarik Award as the best defensive player in the country.

An interception by Eric Collier (33) in the final minute of play destroyed Illinois' hopes of upsetting the Wildcats.

That Championship Season

D'Wayne Bates scored NU's first touchdown on a 34-yard reception.

ROAD TO THE ROSE BOWL

Wildcats' football success brings added interest in NU

BY MIKE LOPRESTI
USA Today

EVANSTON, Ill., Dec. 15, 1995 – What's a Rose Bowl trip worth?

The high command at Northwestern is not yet sure.

• Admissions. There was a 23 percent jump in early applications this fall. Phone inquiries have been heavy, especially Mondays after weekend games. Rebecca Dixon, associate provost of university enrollment, said the final total probably won't be much changed from previous years.

• Alumni development. Vice president Ronald Vanden Dorpel said the school raised $101 million last year. Since 1987, 17 mega-donors have contributed at least $5 million each. When the university needed $90 million for the rather unromantic job of renovating the engineering building – "Steam pipes and asbestos removal is not sexy stuff" – it brought in $93 million.

But he is expecting a boon in contributions to the athletic department, an area traditionally lacking. "I'm certain of this," he said. "It will not be robbing Peter to pay Paul. What we have engendered here is new money, new gifts."

Vanden Dorpel's office has added fax machines and phones to make all the Rose Bowl arrangements for Northwestern's well heeled and fired-up alumni. The school will charter 160 buses for alumni arriving in southern California. A New Year's Eve reception for major donors will be held at the Nixon Library.

Northwestern has sent more stars in to the entertainment industry than to the N.F.L. There's a photo of young Ann-Margret in the chorus line of a school musical. Charlton Heston recently asked that a box of Northwestern shirts be mailed out for the party.

• Public relations. "It's not often," media relations manager Charles Loebbaka said, "that I talk to *Time*, *Newsweek*, *U.S. News and World Report* and *People* magazine in the same week."

He has fielded calls from everywhere, including one from the married couple who met on the train to Northwestern's Rose Bowl in 1949 and intend to go back on the train this year.

Northwestern is Paterno's Kind of Team

By Michael Giarrusso
The Associated Press

STATE COLLEGE, Pa., Nov. 1, 1995 — If Penn State weren't playing Northwestern on Saturday, Joe Paterno would be rooting for the sixth-ranked Wildcats.

"As a coach, I believe in exactly the way they're doing things," Paterno said. "I won't have any fun this Saturday, but I've enjoyed watching a couple of their games on tape. They'd be my kind of team."

For three years, Paterno has been saying Gary Barnett would turn around the Northwestern program. Now that the Wildcats (7-1, 5-0 in the Big Ten) have a shot at the Rose Bowl, people are starting to believe him.

"If they can get in it without beating us, I'd be happy for them," Paterno said. "All of us who feel strongly about what college football can mean to an institution are pleased to see what's happened at Northwestern. They're a fine academic institution and they have not lowered their academic standards and they're still very competitive."

No. 12 Penn State (6-2, 3-2 in the Big Ten) is a slight favorite to beat the Wildcats.

When the Nittany Lions take the field in Evanston, Paterno may think he's playing against one of Penn State's great teams of the past.

"They remind me a lot of my good teams," he said. "They've stayed healthy, they're very disciplined, they're very smart, they play team defense, they play team offense, they hang onto the football, they don't make a lot of mistakes in the kicking game and they don't have a lot of foolish penalties."

The turnaround at Northwestern may end up as dramatic as what happened at Colorado when Barnett was an assistant. Colorado went from 1-10 to a national title in six seasons.

"When I look at his teams, it was never a get-rich-quick scheme," Paterno said. "They had a plan, they stuck with it and they've gotten better."

Wide receiver Freddie Scott said he doesn't relish going into Northwestern ranked behind the Wildcats.

"I have a couple friends from high school playing there and I'm sure they'll be rubbing that in my face all week," he said.

Defensive end Terry Killens wasn't that surprised by Northwestern's success.

"I thought last year they had a pretty sound squad," he said. "They played us tough except for a couple of mistakes."

Penn State beat Northwestern, 45-17, last season, but the Wildcats outgained the Nittany Lions, 475 yards to 341. Northwestern turned the ball over four times, including a fumble that Kim Herring returned 80 yards for a touchdown.

Northwestern is not as mistake prone this year. The Wildcats lead the nation in turnover ratio with 26 takeaways and just seven turnovers.

"They base a lot of their success on their ability to create turnovers," Paterno said. "If we're going to have any success against them, we have to prevent them from creating some turnovers against us."

Northwestern has come so far that Penn State is now trying to live up to the example being set by the Wildcats.

"It's kind of a role reversal," Killens said.

"When you look at them, you see a lot of things that I hope people see in us," Paterno said.

CHAPTER 11

Wildcats field general Steve Schnur (10) launches an aerial strike against the Nittany Lions.

Cats Continue to Roll

NU Victory Train Leaves Lions at Station

BY THOMAS GEORGE
Special to The New York Times

EVANSTON, Ill., Nov. 4, 1995 — Looking much like a team fully aware of the potential glory ahead while distancing itself from the ashes behind, Northwestern continued climbing the mountain today. The Wildcats have taken on all serious comers now, among the best the Big Ten has to offer, including last season's conference and Rose Bowl champion.

That would be Penn State. Include that bunch now as another stop for the Northwestern Express, much like Notre Dame and Michigan and Wisconsin were.

Because when Northwestern defeated Penn State, 21–10, at rocking Dyche Stadium this afternoon, the Wildcats moved oh–so close to a possible Big Ten banner, the Rose Bowl and, at the very least, a New Year's Day bowl appearance.

Now Northwestern (8-1 overall, 6-0 in the Big Ten) must defeat Iowa at home and win at Purdue and hope Ohio State loses or ties one of its remaining games. If that happens, Northwestern's gaudy purple and white will be in the Rose Bowl.

And even if Ohio State gets to go to Pasadena by virtue of its better overall record, Wildcat purple is likely to regain in another bowl on New Year's Day. The Wildcats are that close. The sellout crowd of 49,256 in brisk 30–degree weather left no doubt about that. Fans stormed the field afterward, celebrating joyously.

"Anytime you see anyone play the game of football the way they did today you've got to admire it," Penn State coach Joe Paterno said. "They have great cohesion. They don't have a lot of glamour, except for Autry. They don't go out and glamour you, they just plod along. Nothing spectacular. They're my kind of team."

Wildcat running back Darnell Autry helped place his team on the threshold of something special. He ran hard and wild again today, scoring three touchdowns, the third a 1-yard run with 11 minutes 3 seconds remaining that turned a close game (14-10) into an impossible one (21-10) for Penn State.

The Nittany Lions are now 6-3 and have learned, like the rest of the Big Ten, that Northwestern is a determined and talented club.

"We've got talent," Autry said, wincing when someone asked if the Wildcats were less talented than some of the teams they have beaten. "We've got heart and talent. I wasn't looking into the eyes of the Penn State players to see if they respected us. I was playing my game."

What a game. Thirty-six carries for 139 yards with a long run of 23 yards. Rushing scores of 2 and 10 yards in the first half that helped Northwestern build a 14-7 halftime lead.

And the Northwestern drive that put the game away was a strong indication of its resolve. After both teams had missed field goals and blown other scoring chances late, Northwestern seemed to say, enough. It offered an 80-yard, 9-play drive early in the fourth quarter with Autry scoring to seal it.

The drive was well-planned and focused, including a sneaky reverse run that kept things going. All along the way, Northwestern seemed to be signaling that this series was the game. Northwestern approached it that way, in such a workmanlike manner that when Autry scored, you could almost hear the piercing sigh of disgust and hope lost from the Penn State sideline.

"We must be pretty good," Northwestern coach Gary Barnett said. "We tried to start a new season in November. Champions are crowned in November."

After Autry's running put Northwestern ahead, 14-0, Penn State closed to within 14-7 on Wally Richardson's 5-yard bullet pass to tight end Keith Olsommer. Penn State scored the only points in the third quarter — a Brett Conway 25-yard field goal — and it was 14-10 entering the final period. In the third, Penn State had the ball for nearly 11 minutes. Autry said his club knew that once it got it back, it had better put this game away.

Northwestern did.

Quarterback Steve Schnur (10 of 16, 96 yards) was steady. On defense, Northwestern entered allowing 12.8 points per game and did even better than that against Penn State. Penn State, with all of that size, all of the skill, all of the history, all of that big-play ability, was shut down. The Nittany Lions' longest run was for 20 yards. Their longest pass was for 19 yards. The Northwestern cornerbacks, Chris Martin (one interception) and Rodney Ray, played daring and sticky man-to-man coverage, preventing big plays and allowing the Wildcats to use more punch on their blitz packages. Penn State wide receiver Bobby Engram's numbers said it all: four catches for 46 yards, with a long catch of just 18 yards.

"We were flying around and making big plays instead of hoping to make them," Northwestern linebacker Pat Fitzgerald said. "It's all hype who is good and who is not coming out of high school. We play the kind of defense where we keep everything in front of us. When we do that, we're pretty good."

So much is in front of Northwestern now. So much is behind them. A rosy picture all the way around.

Northwestern 21
Penn State 10

Penn State	0	7	3 0-10
Northwestern	7	7	0 7-21

NU: Autry 2-yard run (Gowins kick)
NU: Autry 10-yard run (Gowins kick)
PSU: Olsommer 5-yard pass from Richardson (Conway kick)
PSU: FG Conway 24 yards
NU: Autry 1-yard run (Gowins kick)
A: 49,256

	PSU	NU
First downs	15	16
Rushes-yards	38-103	43-168
Passing	129	96
Return yards	1	9
Comp-att-int	18-29-1	10-16-1
Punts	6-39	4-36
Fumbles-lost	0-0	2-1
Penalties-yards	7-65	5-35
Time of possession	33:53	26:07

RUSHING: Penn St., Pitts 14-44, Whitman 7-38, Milne 3-22, Enis 4-11, Archie 3-9, Richardson 7-(minus 21). Northwestern, D. Autry 36-139, Beazley 1-25, A. Autry 1-9, Schnur 5-(minus 5).
PASSING: Penn St., Richardson 18-29-1-129. Northwestern, Schnur 10-16-1-96.
RECEIVING: Penn St., Engram 4-46, Scott 4-39, Olsonmmer 3-13, Whitman 3-3, Archie 3-26, Milne 1-2. Northwestern, Bates 4-52, Drexler 3-28, Musso 1-16, Hartl 1-1, Graham 1-(minus 1).

ROAD TO THE ROSE BOWL

Darnell Autry reads the Penn State defense before heading upfield. He was a battering ram against the Nittany Lions, scoring three touchdowns.

That Championship Season

Wide receiver Dave Beazley (86) rips through the Penn State defense for a 25-yard jaunt.

Road to the Rose Bowl

That Championship Season

Dream Comes True Again for Northwestern

By T.J. Simers
Special to The Los Angeles Times

EVANSTON, Ill., Nov. 5, 1995 — Beyond the purple haze there looms more magic: Ohio State loses to Michigan, Florida State tops Florida, Tennessee folds, and Nebraska is unable to bail out enough players to field a team.

Northwestern wins the national championship, Charlton Heston plays the made-for-TV movie role of Wildcat coach Gary Barnett and youngsters everywhere dream of going to college for a good education and the chance to be just like Darnell Autry.

Is there anything more unbelievable than this: Northwestern has now defeated Notre Dame, Michigan and Penn State in the same year. That has never happened here before in the same decade, but Saturday at Dyche Stadium, the sixth-ranked Wildcats nailed the trifecta with a 21-10 victory over Joe Paterno and his 12th-ranked Nittany Lions before 49,256.

"You stand on the sideline and you think back to games when you played out there and there were 15,000 people at the game," Steve Schnur said. "And then you look up and there are 40,000 purple fans going crazy, and it's just an awesome thing."

The Wildcats (8-1, 6-0 in the Big Ten) upset Notre Dame and Michigan on the road, but on this day their swelling faithful enjoyed Northwestern's biggest home victory since defeating the Irish, 35-6, in 1962.

The party has been a long time in coming, and after Schnur knelt down to run out the clock and secure the victory, the fans stormed the field and began climbing the goal posts. A chant of "Rose Bowl, Rose Bowl" had already been raised, and while Ohio State must lose for Northwestern to go to Pasadena, it's the first time since 1948 that those words had any significant meaning around here.

"People just don't seem to want to admit they're a good team, but I'm telling you they are good," Paterno said. "They don't have a lot of glamour athletes

ROAD TO THE ROSE BOWL

Darnell Autry (24) dives for a 1-yard touchdown in the fourth quarter to seal the Wildcats' 21-10 victory.

That Championship Season

and, like some of the good teams I had over the years, they don't do anything fancy or win big. They just win. They don't look spectacular doing it, but they're my kind of football team."

The Wildcats, while short on household names, feature a sophomore running back in Autry who should get Heisman Trophy attention. For the 10th consecutive game, Autry topped the 100 yard mark, and in rushing for 147 yards in 36 carries with three touchdowns, he did so against the nation's 13th-best rushing defense.

"I'm sure they were gearing up to stop the run," Autry said, "but if the offensive line is doing their job, then I don't think it matters."

Northwestern won the coin toss and broke from college tradition. Instead of deferring to the second half, they opted to take the football. It had all been planned before the game.

"It was partly psychological and it was partly done because we wanted one more offensive possession if we could get it," Barnett said. "We wanted our offense on the field."

The Northwestern offense is Autry left and Autry right. Autry, who ran for 171 yards against Penn State last year in his first collegiate start, gave Northwestern a 14-0 lead with touchdown runs of 2 and 10 yards before closing the scoring with a 1-yard dive in the fourth quarter.

"The final drive was just good stuff," Autry said.

"Obviously no one is giving us respect for having good athletes, but if you look at that last scoring drive you saw how focused we are as a team."

Penn State (6-3, 3-3 in the Big Ten), which made a pitch for momentum with a touchdown in the closing seconds of the first half, limited the Wildcats to three offensive plays in the third quarter. The game

THE AUTRY FILE

Tailback Darnell Autry carried 36 times for 139 yards and three touchdowns in a 21-10 victory over Penn State to continue his rewriting of the Northwestern record books. Here are his NU records:

- Rushed for more than 100 yards for the 10th consecutive game.
- Posted his 11th career 100-yard rushing game, tying Autry for the NU record set by Dennis Lundy last season.
- Ran his season point total to 84, breaking the mark of 80 set by Bob Christian in 1990.
- Scored three touchdowns to run his season total to 14, erasing Ron Burton's mark of 12 set in 1958.
- Ran his season rushing total to 1,339 yards, erasing Christian's mark of 1,291 in 1989.
- Set NU record by scoring two or more touchdowns in five games this season. Christian (1989) and Burton (1958) each had four.

began to tilt in favor of the Lions, but after closing to 14-10 on Brett Conway's 24-yard goal, Penn State self-destructed.

"We had our opportunities," Paterno said, "But that's the best defense we have played this season."

The Lions controlled the ball for 8:17 but failed to score when Conway's 27-yard field-goal attempt was ruled wide right. Penn State argued the call, but Northwestern took the ball and Barnett called a team meeting.

"We needed to take the heat off our defense," Barnett said. "We needed a patented 80-yard march, and that's what I told the offense."

Patented? Northwestern has a patent on 80-yard marches? '

The Mildcats?

The Mildcats no more. Northwestern went 80 yards on nine plays, helped in part by wide receiver Dave Beazley's 25-yard run off a reverse on first and 19, to score on Autry's 1-yard run and put Penn State away.

"People talk about Northwestern being this and that, but that's the past," said Wildcat linebacker Pat Fitzgerald, who had a team-high 20 tackles. "We don't know anything about the past; this is our time."

It began with Notre Dame the first week of September, and as Barnett said after the game it continued the first week of October with a victory over Michigan and now the glow of victory once again in this first week of November.

Barnett was asked about the first week of January.

"Something has been mentioned to the team," Barnett said, but as for the rest of the nation, he added, "We'll probably still be underdogs next week against Iowa."

 That Championship Season

ROAD TO THE ROSE BOWL

One Slip Taints Wildcats' Rose Bowl Run

By WILLIAM N. WALLACE
The New York Times

NEW YORK, Nov. 6, 1995 — A low pass from center got by the punter and rolled 36 yards backward to the Northwestern 1-yard line. Miami of Ohio took over there, and as the final gun sounded Chad Seitz kicked a 20-yard field goal to give the Redskins a 30-28 victory.

That botched punt on Sept. 16 may remain the only stain on Northwestern's astounding season, which continued Saturday with a 21-10 victory over Penn State, the defending Big Ten champion. It is an indelible stain, however.

It's likely that on Jan. 1 the Wildcats will play not in the Rose Bowl but in the Florida Citrus Bowl at Orlando, as the No. 2 team in the Big Ten against the Southeastern Conference's No. 2, likely to be either Arkansas or Florida. Unbeaten Ohio State remains in the way of greater glory for Northwestern.

Nebraska is now ranked No. 1 among college football's Top 25 by The New York Times computer,

(Left) Chris Martin (16) celebrates after stopping Penn State's Brian Milne. He later sailed down the sidelines following an interception return (above).

Autry & Co. scored early and often against Penn State. The win boosted NU to a No. 5 ranking.

breaking last week's tie with Florida, and remained atop The Associated Press and USA Today/CNN polls.

The Times computer was more impressed by the Cornhuskers' 73-14 knockout of Iowa State than Florida's 58-20 rout of Northern Illinois, even though the computer collapses runaway scores. The Gators are now second in the computer ranking, followed by Tennessee, Ohio State and Northwestern.

Northwestern (8-1 overall, 6-0 in the Big Ten) has games remaining against Iowa (5-3) and Purdue (3-4-1), the latter a 38-27 upset winner Saturday over Wisconsin. Ohio State (9-0, 5-0 in the Big Ten), which trounced Minnesota, 49-21, Saturday night at Minneapolis, must play Illinois (4-4); Indiana (2-6) and Michigan (7-2).

Northwestern's hopes that the Wolverines might be good enough to upend the Buckeyes on Nov. 25 were darkened after Michigan State upset Michigan, 28-25, a defeat that dropped Michigan from No. 9 to No. 13 in The Times' ranking.

So it is easy to project Ohio State as finishing its season undefeated and tied with Northwestern atop the Big Ten at 8-0. But the conference's first tiebreaker is overall record, and so that loss to Miami of Ohio would cost the Wildcats the trip to the Rose Bowl as Big Ten champion, a trip no Northwestern team has made since the 1948 season.

Penn State's Joe Paterno had compliments for the Wildcats. "They're my kind of team," he said. "Nothing fancy. They don't win big. They just win."

The success of Gary Barnett's Wildcats in 1995 was heralded as a miracle by the media, which attracted a large legion of new followers.

THAT CHAMPIONSHIP SEASON

With a 21-10 lead in the closing moments of the fourth quarter, Fred Wilkerson (26) and the NU players on the sideline got started early on the victory celebration.

ROAD TO THE ROSE BOWL

That Championship Season

The Wildcats join in singing the NU fight song in the locker room following the Penn State game. Four years of hard work led up to this special moment.

Top 25 polls

(For the week of Nov. 5, 1995)

#	The New York Times		Associated Press		USA Today/CNN	
1.	Nebraska	9-0-0	Nebraska	9-0-0	Nebraska	9-0-0
2.	Florida	8-0-0	Ohio State	9-0-0	Ohio State	9-0-0
3.	Tennessee	8-1-0	Florida	8-0-0	Florida	8-0-0
4.	Ohio State	9-0-0	Tennessee	8-1-0	Tennessee	8-1-0
5.	**Northwestern**	**8-1-0**	**Northwestern**	**8-1-0**	**Northwestern**	**8-1-0**
6.	Notre Dame	8-2-0	Florida State	7-1-0	Florida State	7-1-0
7.	Florida State	7-1-0	Kansas State	8-1-0	Kansas State	8-1-0
8.	Kansas State	8-1-0	Notre Dame	8-2-0	Texas	6-1-1
9.	Colorado	7-2-0	Colorado	7-2-0	Notre Dame	8-2-0
10.	Kansas	8-1-0	Kansas	8-1-0	Colorado	7-2-0
11.	Texas	6-1-1	Texas	6-1-1	Southern Cal	7-1-1
12.	Virginia Tech	7-2-0	Southern Cal	7-1-1	Kansas	8-1-0
13.	Michigan	7-2-0	Michigan	7-2-0	Virginia	7-3-0
14.	Southern Cal	7-1-1	Virginia	7-3-0	Texas A&M	5-2-0
15.	San Diego State	7-2-0	Arkansas	7-2-0	Michigan	7-2-0
16.	Arkansas	7-2-0	Alabama	7-2-0	Arkansas	7-2-0
17.	Brigham Young	5-3-0	Oregon	7-2-0	Oregon	7-2-0
17.	Cincinnati	5-4-0	Texas A&M	5-2-0	Alabama	7-2-0
19.	Oregon	7-2-0	Penn State	6-3-0	Virginia Tech	7-2-0
20.	Alabama	7-2-0	Auburn	6-3-0	Auburn	6-3-0
21.	Virginia	7-3-0	Virginia Tech	7-2-0	Penn State	6-3-0
22.	Washington	5-3-1	Washington	5-3-1	Syracuse	6-2-0
23.	Toledo	8-0-1	Syracuse	6-2-0	Washington	5-3-1
24.	U.C.L.A.	6-3-0	Clemson	6-3-0	U.C.L.A.	6-3-0
25.	Auburn	6-3-0	San Diego State	7-2-0	Clemson	6-3-0

Chapter 12

Dreaming of Roses

Cats Defeat Iowa, 31-20, in Journey to Pasadena

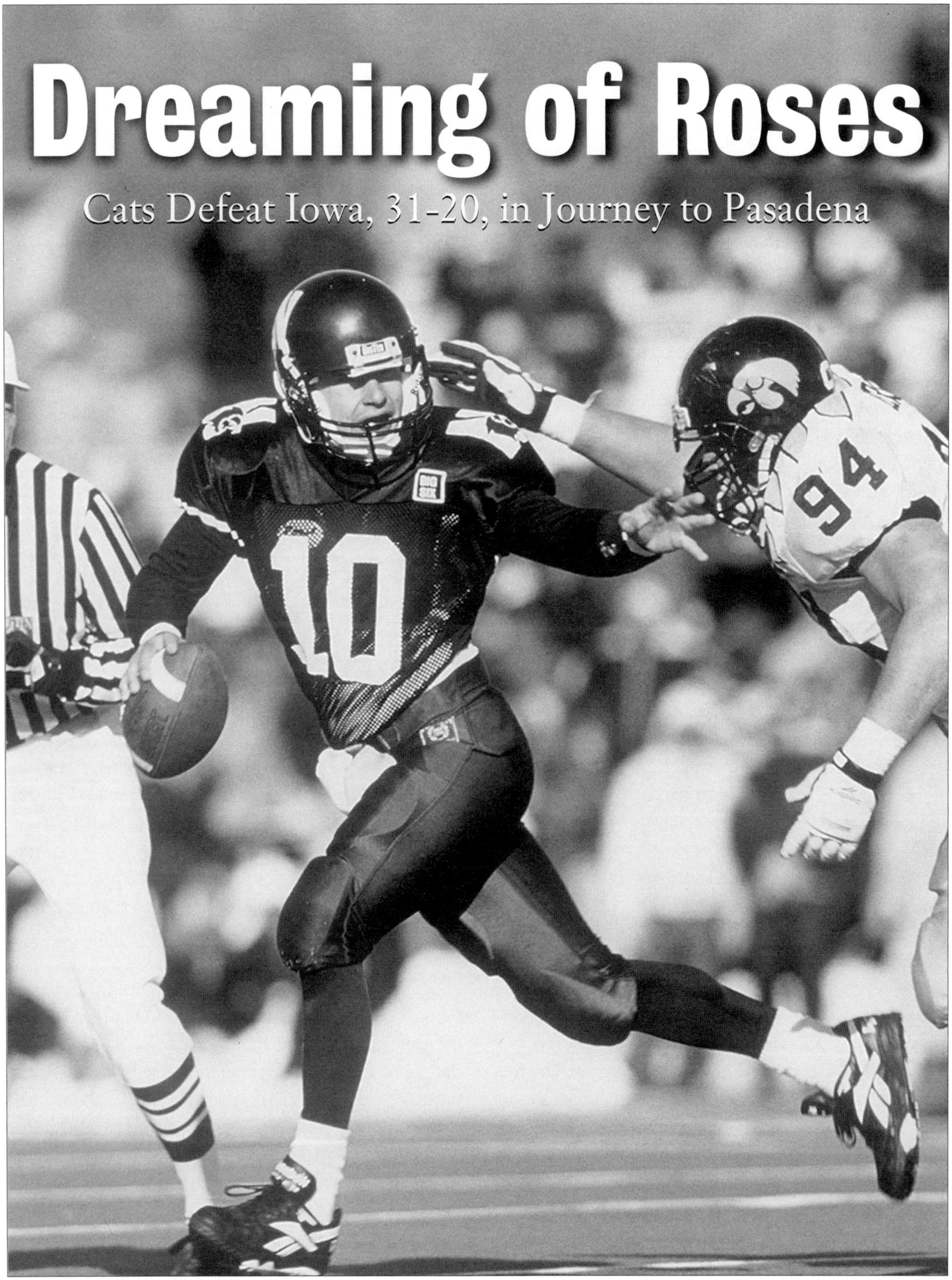

That Championship Season

By Rick Gano
The Associated Press

EVANSTON, Ill., Nov. 11, 1995 — The icy winds were not nearly as numbing to Northwestern as the possibility of losing Saturday. The Wildcats couldn't let it happen.

Not with the warm breezes of the Rose Bowl still beckoning in this improbable season that has been the most surprising in college football.

"We've been down before and have faced pressure before. This was no different. We buckled down," said tailback Darnell Autry, who helped the fifth-ranked Wildcats rally for a 31-20 victory over Iowa, keeping them in the running for a trip to Pasadena.

"They did what they've been doing all year, they found a way to win," said Iowa coach Hayden Fry, whose team led at the half on a frigid day at Dyche Stadium. "It was a typical game for them, they took advantage of opportunities."

Northwestern (9-1, 7-0 in the Big Ten), matching its only other nine-win season in 1903, pitched a second-half shutout at the determined Hawkeyes, scoring the clinching touchdown on Hudhaifa Ismaeli's 31-yard fumble return with 2:56 left.

And Autry, who graced the cover of *Sports Illustrated* this week, gained 100 yards for the 11th straight game and scored the go-ahead touchdown in the third quarter.

The Wildcats' victory, however, was marred by the loss of linebacker Pat Fitzgerald, the top tackler in the Big Ten, who suffered a broken leg in the third quarter and is out for the season finale at Purdue next week and probably for the Wildcats' first bowl trip since 1949. Fitzgerald's injury was initially reported to be a sprained ankle.

"We lost one heck of a player," said Wildcats coach Gary Barnett. "We all have to play a little better. Don Holmes will have to step up and he will."

Northwestern, winning its school-record eighth straight game, also ended a 21-game stretch of futility against Iowa, beating the Hawkeyes for the first time since 1973.

"They will make a good Big Ten bowl representative," said Fry, who denied during the week suggestions that he'd run up the score on the Wildcats over the years.

Northwestern's last nine-win season 92 years ago came against a schedule that included North Division High School, Chicago Dental and Notre Dame.

The game-time temperature Saturday was 26 degrees with a 1-degree wind chill and wind gusting at 30 mph. Plows had to roll a slight snow cover off the artificial turf before the game.

Northwestern, trailing 20-17 at the half, regained the lead with a quick 69-yard drive to begin the third quarter. In the fourth, Ismaeli scooped up a fumble by Iowa tight end Derek Price, after a hit by Rodney Ray, and ran it in.

"The defensive back just made a good play. He put his helmet on the ball in the right spot," Price said. "I just wish I had it back."

Autry's 3-yard touchdown run capped the drive opening the second half, which also featured a 22-yard pass from Steve Schnur to D'Wayne Bates and a 16-yard carry on a reverse by Bates. Autry finished with 110 yards on 32 carries.

Iowa (5-4, 2-4 in the Big Ten) then ate up the rest of the quarter with an 18-play drive that started at its 18 and ended at the Wildcats 30. Hawkeyes quarterback Matt Sherman slipped for a loss on second down and then threw incomplete on the next two, ending the drive.

Northwestern 31
Iowa 20

Iowa	0	20	0	0-20
Northwestern	3	14	7	7-31

NU: FG Gowins 50 yards
Iowa: Shaw 1-yard run (Bromert kick)
Iowa: Knight 28-yard interception return (Bromert kick)
NU: Drexler 21-yard pass from Schnur (Gowins kick)
NU: Musso 60-yard punt return (Gowins kick)
Iowa: Slutzker 39-yard pass from Sherman (kick failed)
NU: D. Autry 3-yard run (Gowins kick)
NU: Ismaeli 31-yard fumble return (Gowins kick)
A: 49,256

	Iowa	NU
First downs	18	11
Rushes-yards	50-145	38-106
Passing	158	82
Return yards	24	60
Comp-att-int	16-24-1	6-12-1
Punts	6-37	6-41
Fumbles-lost	3-1	0-0
Penalties-yards	5-34	4-46
Time of possession	34:55	25:05

RUSHING: Iowa, Shaw 38-135, Burger 6-30, Dwight 1-7, Sherman 5-(minus 27). Northwestern, D. Autry 32-110, Bates 1-16, Schnur 5-(minus 20).
PASSING: Iowa, Sherman 16-23-1-158, Dwight 0-1-0-0. Northwestern, Schnur 6-12-1-82.
RECEIVING: Iowa, Slutzker 5-86, Price 3-12, Shaw 2-9, Burger 2-23, Odems 1-9, Dwight 1-5, Carter 1-9, Guy 1-5. Northwestern, Beazley 2-34, Bates 2-37, Drexler 1-21, D. Autry 1-(minus 10).

(Left to right) Mike Warren (68), Larry Curry (89), Matt Rice (95) and Ray Robey (96) are just a few of the reasons that NU's defense became one of the most feared in the country in 1995.

That Championship Season

Injured NU kicker Sam Valenzisi joins teammates William Bennett (20) and Rob Johnson (57) for the pregame coin toss prior to the Iowa contest.

That Championship Season

Hudhaifa Ismaeli is greeted by Eric Collier (33) following his 31-yard fumble return for a touchdown.

Sedrick Shaw gained 135 yards on 38 carries to go over 1,000 yards and become Iowa's career rushing leader, passing Tony Stewart. He had 93 yards on 26 carries in the first half.

Iowa took a 20-17 halftime lead when Scott Slutzker grabbed a fourth-and-4 pass and dragged Northwestern's Eric Collier into the end zone for a 39-yard touchdown with 1:31 left in the half. But the Hawkeyes' Zach Bromert missed the extra point attempt after a high snap, leaving Northwestern within a field goal.

Northwestern fell behind, 14-3, when Iowa's Tom Knight picked off a pass that deflected off the Wildcats' Matt Hartl and returned it 28 yards for a touchdown with 8:25 left in the second quarter.

Northwestern scored twice in the span of 1 minute 39 seconds to take the lead.

Autry, bottled up most of the half, went for 27 yards and the Wildcats moved 70 yards with Darren Drexler catching a fourth-down pass from Schnur and taking

Brian Musso's 60-yard punt return in the second quarter put the Wildcats ahead, 17-14.

it 21 yards to make it 14-10.

Iowa was stopped, punted and Brian Musso fielded the kick, made an initial fake and then broke free for a 60-yard touchdown, putting the Wildcats ahead 17-14.

Iowa, cheered by a large contingent of bundled-up fans, regained the lead with an 80-yard drive, its second of the half, in eight plays.

Shaw carried 14 times for 54 yards on Iowa's first scoring drive, capping it with a 1-yard run for the touchdown.

Northwestern cut it to 7-3 when Brian Gowins hit a 50-yard field goal.

Iowa lost linebacker Eric Hilgenberg to a knee injury in the first half and fullback Rodney Filer was hurt on the game's first scrimmage play.

(Right) The Cats received an unexpected jolt when Pat Fitzgerald (51) broke his left leg in the third quarter. (Below) NU's win over Iowa ended a 21-year losing streak and gave Wildcat fans a reason to party.

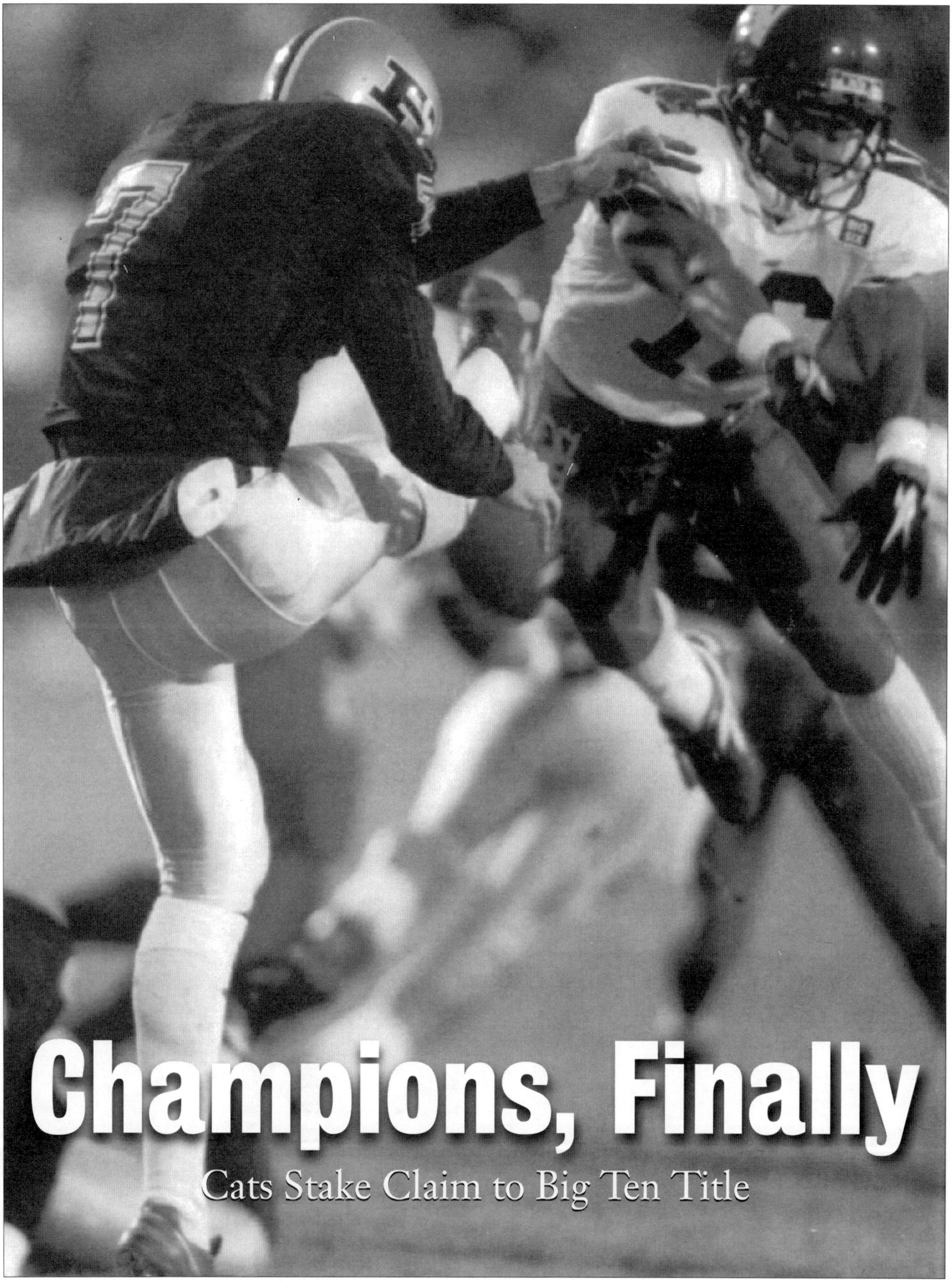

Chapter 13

Champions, Finally
Cats Stake Claim to Big Ten Title

By Hank Lowenkron
The Associated Press

WEST LAFAYETTE, Ind., Nov. 18, 1995 — Northwestern has a share of its first Big Ten title since 1936 and now all the Wildcats can do is wait to see if they're headed to the Rose Bowl or some other bowl game.

With leading tackler Pat Fitzgerald sidelined by two broken bones, Northwestern's defense made up for the loss, and the offense just handed the ball to Darnell Autry.

Autry gained a career-high 226 yards as No. 5 Northwestern beat Purdue, 23-8, to keep its Rose Bowl hopes alive.

"Darnell was pretty tough," Northwestern coach Gary Barnett said. "We played as well as we needed to play on offense.

"That's really been our MO all year. D'Wyane Bates made some big catches. Steve Schnur stuck a couple (passes) in."

But it was defense that consistently foiled the Boilermakers.

"Our defense was just dominant the whole game. Our defensive game, the way our guys played up front was beautiful. I don't know what to say," Barnett said.

Autry, whose previous high was 190 yards earlier this season against Air Force, had a 59-yard carry to set up Northwestern's final touchdown. The carry brought the ball to the 1-yard line, where Schnur scored on a quarterback sneak.

The victory in their regular-season finale assured the Wildcats (10-1, 8-0 in the Big Ten) a share of the league title. Northwestern, which has never won 10 games before in the regular season, needs a Michigan upset of Ohio State next Saturday to claim undisputed possession of the conference championship and its first Rose Bowl trip since the 1948 season.

With a victory, the second-ranked Buckeyes (11-0) would go to the Rose Bowl on the basis of a better overall record.

"When I came, I didn't know when, but I knew this would happen," Autry said of the Big Ten title.

"We put all we had into it. We laid it all out on the line and got the job done," he said of Saturday's game.

During a break in the first quarter against Purdue, NU's pride of the trenches huddles on the sideline, waiting for another opportunity to roll over the Boilermakers' defense.

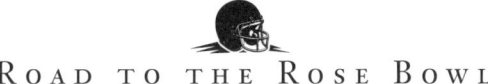

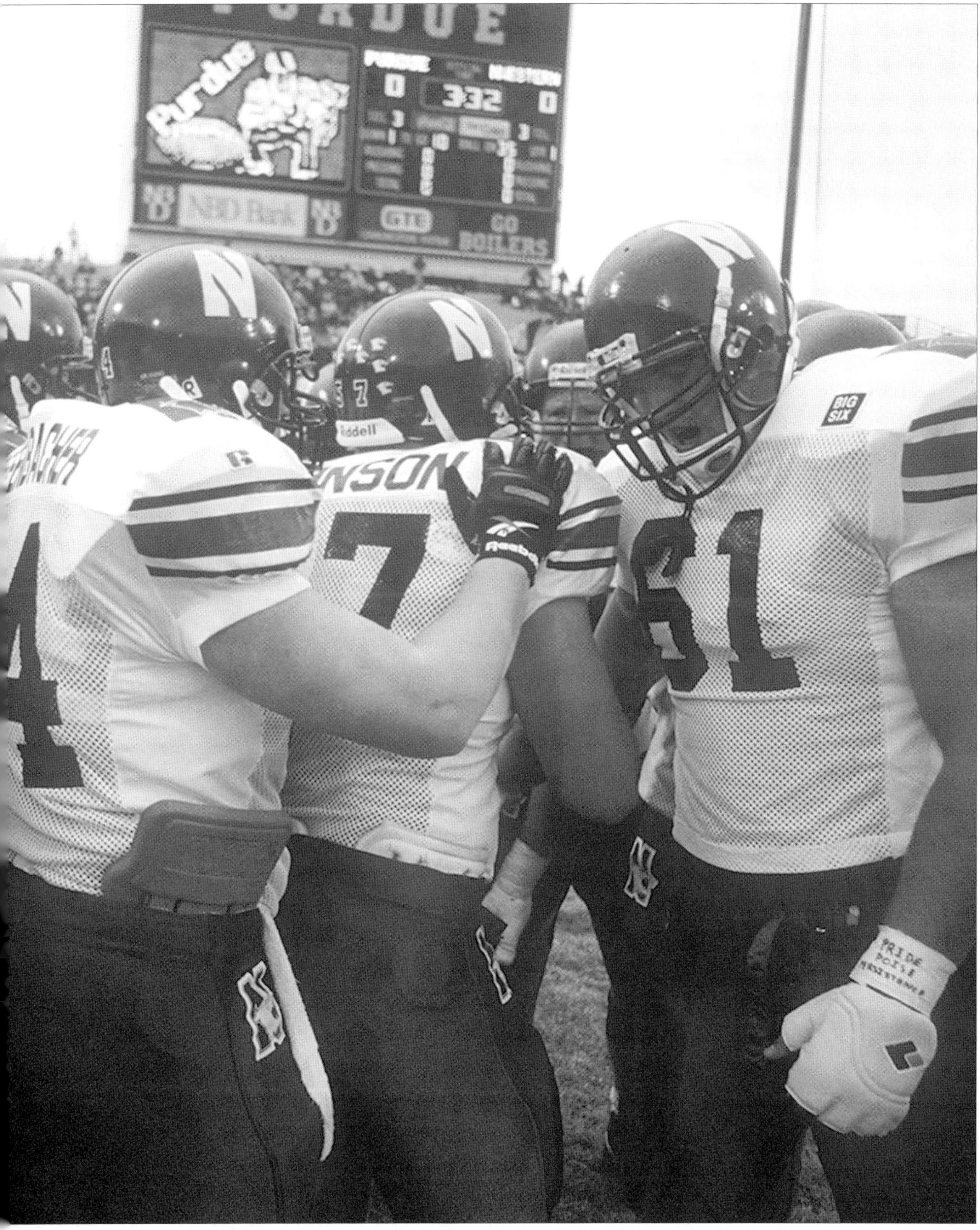
PURDUE
332
GO BOILERS
BIG SIX
Riddell
Reebok
PRIDE

Purdue (3-6-1, 1-5-1 in the Big Ten) never got past Northwestern's 25 until James Coleman blocked a punt deep in Wildcats territory in the fourth quarter. Roosevelt Colvin recovered the ball and brought it to the 9. Two plays later, Edwin Watson scored on a 3-yard run as the Boilermakers avoided being shut out for the second consecutive game and the third time in four outings.

"They came in with a great game plan. They knew that we couldn't get much outside, so they blitzed a lot," said Purdue coach Jim Colletto, whose team was assured of its 12th consecutive losing season.

Autry, the only N.C.A.A. Division I back to gain 100 yards in every game this season, increased his rushing total to 1,675 yards this season.

Meanwhile, fullback Mike Alstott became Purdue's career rushing leader by gaining 71 yards on 16 carries. That gave him 3,371, topping the mark of 3,315 set by Otis Armstrong (1970-72).

"At the time I broke the record it was great," said Alstott, who was presented with the game ball. "After that moment, it was a disappointing game. Things didn't go our way."

Northwestern's defense came up with two scoring plays.

"They all played at a higher level," Barnett said of his defense reacting to the loss of Fitzgerald, who watched the game on crutches along the sideline.

Don Holmes, who started in place of Fitzgerald, had a team-leading 12 tackles.

"Holmes did a good job. It's a defensive team. That's how we played all year," Barnett said.

BIG TEN CHAMPS

Northwestern clinched a share of the Big Ten title, its sixth since 1903:

Year	Conference	Overall
1995	8-0	10-1
1936	6-0	7-1
1931*	5-1	7-1-1
1930*	5-0	7-1
1926*	5-0	7-1
1903*	1-0-2	9-2-3

*Co-champions

Northwestern 23
Purdue 8

Northwestern	7	7	9	0—23
Purdue	0	0	0	8—8

NU: Martin 76-yard pass interception return (Gowins kick)
NU: Bates 72-yard pass from Schnur (Gowins kick)
NU: Safety, Deigman tackled in end zone
NU: Schnur 1-yard run (Gowins kick)
Pur: Watson 3-yard run (Alsott pass from Trefzger)
A: 47,172

	NU	Pur
First downs	14	16
Rushes-yards	44-211	38-123
Passing	158	178
Return yards	113	20
Comp-att-int	12-21-1	22-37-2
Punts	6-33	7-32
Fumbles-lost	2-1	5-1
Penalties-yards	1-10	2-15
Time of possession	29:33	30:27

RUSHING: Northwestern, D. Autry 32-226, A. Autry 3-3, Schnur 5-3, Leary 3-(Minus 3), Brown 1-(Minus 19). Purdue, Alstott 13-71, Watson 9-32, Rogers 6-22, L. Johnson 1-2, Trefzer 9-(minus 4).
PASSING: Northwestern, Schnur, 12-20-1-158, McGrew 0-1-0-0. Purdue, Trefzger 22-37-1-178.
RECEIVING: Northwestern, Bates, 6-131, D. Autry 4-16, Graham 1-6, Hartl 1-5. Purdue, Blackman 8-83, Alstott 6-17, Olivadotti 3-31, Jones 2-14, Allen 2-12, Alford 1-21

Faced with a fourth-and-5 on its first possession at the Northwestern 35, the Boilermakers decided to gamble.

The move backfired when Chris Martin intercepted Rick Trefzger's pass and raced 76 yards for the game's first score.

Chris Koepper also blocked a Purdue punt and tackled the punter in the end zone for a safety in the third quarter. After the ensuing kick by Purdue, Autry had his long run.

The Wildcats wasted a scoring opportunity on their second possession of the game, driving from their 29 to the Purdue 1.

On fourth down, they faked a field goal and fullback Mike McGrew's pass fell incomplete after he took a pitch from holder Paul Burton.

The rest of the first half was mainly a punting contest, with the Boilermakers kicking five times and Northwestern four.

The only other score in the first half came on a 72-yard TD toss from Schnur to D'Wayne Bates, who got behind the defense at the Purdue 45. Bates finished the game with six catches for 131 yards.

Casey Daily (36), Eric Collier and the NU defense kept Boilermaker quarterback Rick Trefzenger on the run all afternoon.

That Championship Season

Darnell Autry (24) scampers down the sideline for 59 yards to set up NU's final touchdown. Autry finished the game with a career-high 226 yards on 32 carries.

That Championship Season

Northwestern Takes a Drink After a Very Long Drought

By Rick Gano
The Associated Press

EVANSTON, Ill., Nov. 19, 1995 — It's been nearly 60 years since their last championship. Most people never expected to see the Northwestern Wildcats atop the Big Ten again. Never.

But here they are, the most surprising team in college football this season. A 10-1 record, the school's first 10-win season, an 8-0 mark in the conference where they were doormats for so long.

Memories of a 34-game losing streak during the 1980s are foggy and distant, nearly erased by the school's first Big Ten title since 1936.

"I wasn't here 60 years ago but people have been stopping me and saying, 'Thank you, thank you. It's been so long,'" said sophomore tailback Darnell Autry, who rushed for 226 yards Saturday as the fourth-ranked Wildcats completed their surprising regular season by beating Purdue, 23-8.

"We've done a lot for our school and we've done a lot for each other," Autry said. "I'm not aware that we're one of the greatest stories in history. But I am aware that we are one of the great teams."

The Wildcats pulled out celebratory shirts and caps Saturday, proclaiming themselves Big Ten champions, even though they might still have to share the title with unbeaten Ohio State.

That's one reason they'll be gathered around television sets Saturday when No. 2 Ohio State plays at No. 18 Michigan. A Michigan win puts Northwestern in the Rose Bowl for the first time since 1949. If Ohio State wins, the Buckeyes go to Pasadena and the Wildcats go to the Citrus Bowl at Orlando, Fla., probably against Tennessee.

"For the first time in my life I'm becoming a Michigan fan," said linebacker Pat Fitzgerald, who is out with a broken leg.

From the bleachers in Ross-Ade Stadium at West Lafayette, Ind., on Saturday, Wildcats players could hear the fans chanting something three months ago no one would have believed could be directed at them: "Big Ten champs!"

"I remember the tough going," said defensive back

Chris Martin, who returned an interception for a touchdown and blocked a punt for a safety Saturday. "We stuck together. It made me feel good to hear our fans like that."

Quarterback Steve Schnur, who threw only five interceptions this season and consistently completed the big passes to supplement the running of Autry, summed up the remarkable season this way:

"Not in my wildest dreams did I expect this. The championship will take some time to sink in but nothing can take this away.

"This is something I will look back on my entire life and for one day, I will be a Michigan fan when they play Ohio State."

Autry, so homesick after last season that he contemplated transferring to be close to his Tempe, Ariz., home, knew that once he returned Northwestern would start winning.

"We believed all along," he said. "And now everyone believes. It was incredible out there ... What a feeling. I'll never forget it."

With a share of the Big Ten title wrapped up, NU coach Gary Barnett meets with the media following the Purdue contest.

That Championship Season

(Above) It doesn't get any better than this! Linebacker Mike Warren (68) leads the post-game singing and toasting in the locker room.
(Right) Guard Ryan Padgett, being congratulated by teammate Rodney Ray (at right), claims ownership of the Big Ten trophy for NU.

Chapter 14

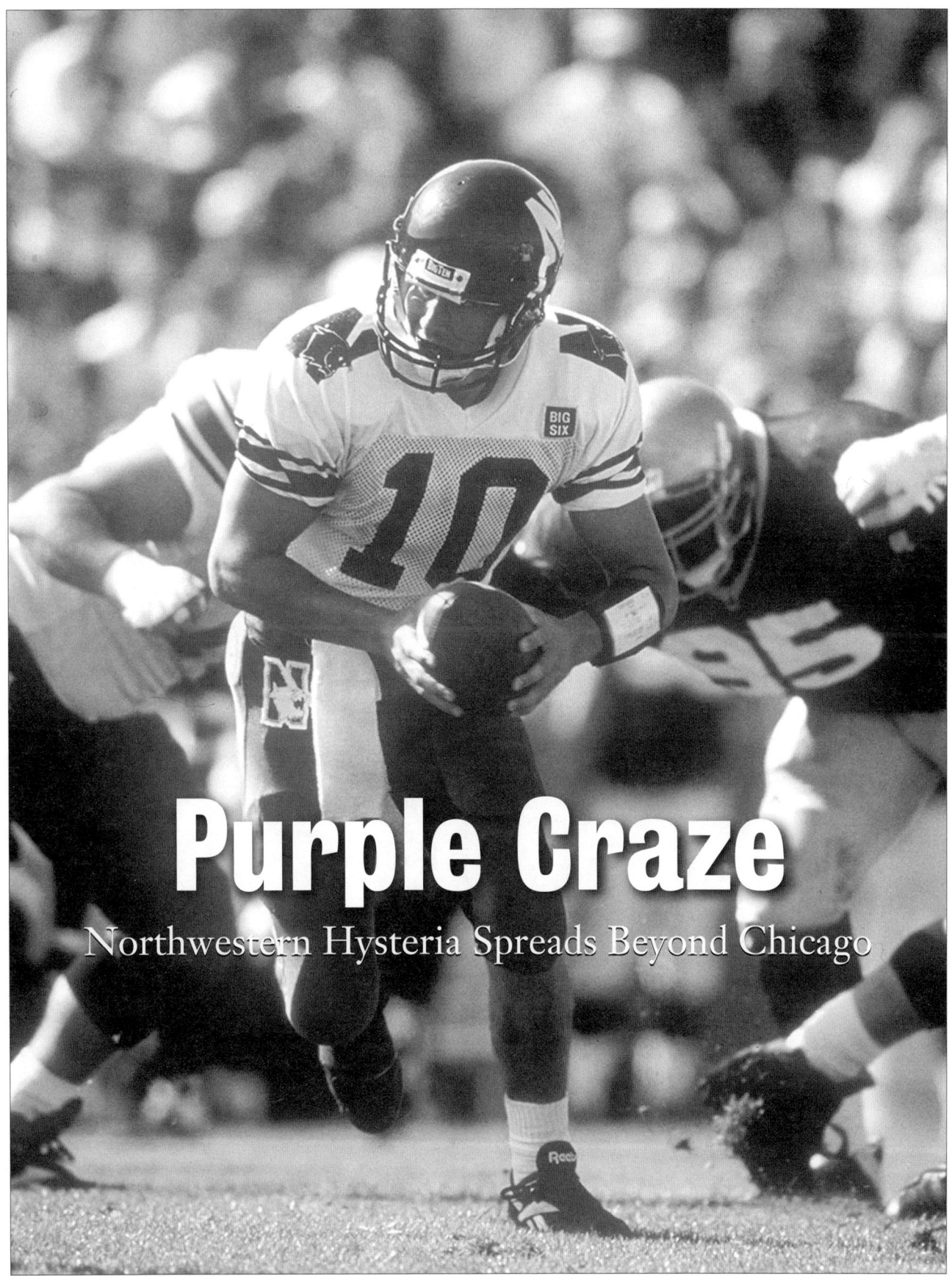

Purple Craze
Northwestern Hysteria Spreads Beyond Chicago

That Championship Season

By John U. Bacon
The Detroit News

EVANSTON, Ill., Dec. 17, 1995 — News brief: The sun now sets in the East, hell just froze over and bears in the woods have switched to port-a-potties.

Now today's big story: Northwestern is playing in the Rose Bowl.

The Wildcats earned their first appearance in the Rose Bowl since 1949 by going undefeated in the Big Ten. In the process, they became the first team since Michigan State in 1965 to beat Notre Dame, Michigan and Penn State in the same year, and they're taking a 10-1 overall mark and a No. 3 national ranking into their Jan. 1 showdown with No. 18 Southern Cal.

OK, perhaps you've heard all that. Everyone loves this story because it's a classic tale of the little engine that could, an inspirational saga of the cute little mom-and-pop operation that bested the established powers at their own game.

As a result, the normally dour Northwestern students, the restrained town of Evanston, Ill., and even the stodgy faculty are discarding their stoic silence for adolescent yelps of joy not heard in these parts since ... well, ever. How else do you explain the problem of Doug Bowers, a 1988 grad who had to choose between attending his grandmother's 90th birthday party and a trip to the Rose Bowl — and very narrowly picked his grandmother's birthday?

Remember: The last time Northwestern prepared to go to the Rose Bowl, President Clinton was 4 and the team took a train.

"The last time we were in the Rose Bowl was 1949," Bowers said. "But Nanna was born in 1905. And there won't be 110,000 screaming, drunken fans at her party. She wins, but I have to admit, it was closer than I let on."

But the story doesn't end there.

"Our identity has done a 180," says Jennifer Brown, a first-year student from San Diego, "and we're just sitting here in the middle watching it spin around."

New Attitude

"Losing so much became sort of a badge of courage," said athletic director Rick Taylor, who left a similar job at the University of Cincinnati two years

The Wildcats' 17-15 win over Notre Dame: It was a day NU players will always remember.

That Championship Season

ago to revive the Northwestern program. Taylor never bought into that. "The university would never allow such failure to continue in any other field, so why ours?"

"Why" isn't clear, but the effects of the slump are obvious. According to the authoritative *Insider's Guide to the Colleges*, Northwestern students' primary social outlet is "going to the library. ... The social scene is very uptight for a large university."

Evanston is a serious-minded, upright town. The Women's Temperance Union, which successfully campaigned for prohibition, originated in Evanston, and local Methodist lay ministers started Northwestern University itself — which might explain why there are 80 churches in a college town of about 70,000. Evanston remained dry until 1972, and even now the few places that sell drinks must serve food.

The buildings on campus reflect this austerity, and come in two styles: neo-gothic limestone or futuristic reinforced concrete. Both have the same dirty white color as the frozen surface of Lake Michigan a block away, and give off about as much warmth.

In short, Evanston is a place that could use a little levity.

So it's a little refreshing to see the former student-drones in line at the campus book store during finals week buying not highlighters, index cards or Cliff's Notes, but Northwestern Rose Bowl stuff by the armfull. Even during finals week, students are more concerned with Rose Bowl tickets than exams — surely a first.

The football bug even caught up with notoriously stodgy professors. A day before the Northwestern-Illinois game, in a highly competitive chemistry course with more than 200 students, an acclaimed professor brought out a flask full of a bright orange solution. After stirring up a second solution while explaining certain chemical reactions, the professor dumped the second batch into the first flask and — shazam! — the Illini-orange solution suddenly burst into Northwestern purple. The lecture hall erupted in cheers.

"The faculty members whom you might have expected to fall into that cynical, bah-humbug mold have not done so," said Frederick Hemke, who's served as the athletic department's faculty representative for 15 years. "A lot of professors who've never talked about athletics in the past have come out of the closet."

Winds of Change

The football team's success has also had a salubrious effect on the school's relations with Evanston, Chicago and even their opponents. City-campus relations have always been a bit strained. As one local said, "Northwestern owns damn near half of Evanston. They don't pay any taxes, but they'll charge you four bucks to sit on their beach."

But since the team's unprecedented roll, "the town's been much nicer to the students," junior Peter Grosz said. And Chicago's been much nicer to the university.

Many locals will tell you Chicago has been searching for a college team to call its own for decades. "Chicago flirted with Notre Dame and Illinois, only due to a lack of another team nearby," Taylor said. "Notre Dame and Illinois are really step-children. (Football Coach) Gary Barnett said before this year, 'If we succeed we'll own Chicago' — and that's proven correct."

It's worth noting that Ann Arbor is twice as far from Detroit as Evanston is from Chicago — and East Lansing is farther — but Michigan and Michigan State have had a stronger gravitational pull on Michigan's biggest city than Northwestern had on Chicago. For decades, Northwestern has touted the virtues of Chicago prominently in its glossy brochures, but in return Chicago newspapers barely mentioned Northwestern.

That's all changed. The same papers that used to give more print to a Notre Dame loss than a Northwestern victory now devote half the front page to headlines like, "CATS WIN BIG TEN."

The long arm of Northwestern hysteria now extends from coast to coast. When

---

Northwestern receiver D'Wayne Bates.

Following Northwestern's 31-20 victory over Iowa, the students stormed the field and attempted to tear down the goal post.

one Northwestern alum boarded a plane in New York City wearing a Wildcats hat, the ticket guy asked where he was sitting. Coach class, he said. The ticket-taker shook his head and said, "Not today, you're not!" and moved him up to first class. Another alum who bet $100 in each of the past 20 years in Las Vegas that Northwestern would win the Big Ten collected a cool $25,000 this year.

Even the Wildcats' opponents are part of the lovefest. One Purdue player admitted that he wanted to hate them, but couldn't muster the malice necessary to do so. Since Michigan's victory over Ohio State got Northwestern into the Rose Bowl, U-M alums are now being received on campus as warmly as the American G.I.s were by liberated Paris.

A University Ambushed

Like the U.S. in World War II, the Northwestern administrators were caught woefully unprepared for recent events, but have mobilized with remarkable swiftness to meet the new demands. The sports information department, for example, printed 5,500 copies of its football media guide, about half as many as Michigan does each year. They have no secretary (Penn State's office has three), and they just got voice mail a few years ago.

"We had no idea — none — of what we were in for," media services director Brad Hurlbut said. "It all started after the Michigan game, and each week tops the one before it. We kept saying it can't get any worse, but we don't say that anymore."

Hurlbut now receives more than 100 calls a day. The day I interviewed him for this story Hurlbut fielded queries from *Ebony* magazine, *Crain's Chicago*, *TV Guide*, *The Sporting News*, *The Fort Worth Star-Telegram*, *Sports Illustrated*, *NBC Nightly News*, *The Associated Press*, *The Washington Post* and *The Tonight Show with Jay Leno* — to name a few.

Much of NU's success is based on the hard work and team spirit that was formed at their summer pre-season camp in Kenosha, Wisconsin.

"We're still waiting to hear from Martha Stewart," Hurlbut said. He laughed, then abruptly stopped laughing.

Because of this onslaught from all sides, stadium security had to relearn its job; the campus phone and e-mail systems were rendered useless for three days after the Rose Bowl invitation; and the ticket office had to fly in three Michigan athletic department staffers to help them handle the deluge of Rose Bowl ticket requests. Their 21,000 ticket allotment vanished in a week.

Mania and Money

John Pearce, the assistant marketing manager for Champion sports apparel, estimates his company has licensing agreements with more than 2,000 universities, "just about every school you can think of," Pearce said. Pearce said he has been impressed with the boom in demand for Northwestern stuff. Last year, Northwestern didn't sell enough merchandise to crack the top 1,000 schools, but this year its sales place them among the top 25 universities. "That's really huge for us," Pearce said.

That's not news to Gail Parseghian, a distant relative of the former Notre Dame coach, who is in charge of licensing at Northwestern. "The number of designs I approved went up 1,250 percent over the previous November. I almost stopped smoking when this started," she said.

Parseghian didn't stop smoking, but she has stopped going out for lunch. It seems no one in Evanston does these days, including Ross Kooperman, the owner and operator of the Locker Room, a T-shirt store across the street from Dyche Stadium. Though the Locker Room isn't big enough to house a basketball team standing up, Kooperman sold 1,400 Big Ten champion hats out of that little shop in nine days, and had 720 more coming in the next day.

"I've been in business three years here," Kooperman said while attending to the never-ending line of customers, "and I just did more business in the first 2 1/2 hours today than I did my whole first month here. I'm getting calls from all over — Singapore, Brazil, you name it. I can tell you there's at least one car in Morocco with a Northwestern bumper sticker on it."

One of Kooperman's helpers is Cynthia Robinson, who says, "My main concern at work used to be remembering to bring my Steely Dan CDs and a good book to read, and once in a while I was interrupted by a customer. This year — pandemonium. We let people in when we open at 10 a.m, and turn customers away when we close at 6."

At the Jones Sweet Shoppe downtown, they can't keep enough purple and white candy in stock. It's outselling the red and white Christmas variety.

The Ripple Effect

With any successful football team, one would reasonably expect this higher demand for tickets and T-shirts. But the depth and breadth of the changes Northwestern's 10-1 season wrought is still surprising.

Consider the Northwestern sailing club, which is now able to solicit more corporate support because of the football team. "They know who we are now," said Beth Holland, a sophomore who makes the calls. "I had to learn Darnell Autry's football stats just to talk with these guys."

Rebecca Dixon is in charge of admissions and financial aid, and she reports that applications for "early decision" are up 23 percent from the previous year. Though that group represents a small sample size, the demand for campus tours has been unusually heavy this fall, and every Monday after football games "our phones are ringing off the hooks," Dixon said. "It's wild around here."

It is surely ironic that the bigger the senior football players, the smarter the freshmen-wannabes. One junior admitted, "I wouldn't want to be in next year's applicant pool."

A Magical Moment in Time

The little engine that could is bound to get bigger in the coming years, if only to accommodate all the new passengers. Wheaties plans to feature a Northwestern football helmet on one of its boxes soon; the suddenly crowded press box will have a priority list for media requests next year; and the school currently is raising $20 million for stadium renovations and a new indoor practice field.

"Given our facilities," university president Henry S. Bienen says, "Gary's been recruiting with one hand tied behind his back."

While Northwestern might be discarding the homey feel of its sports program forever, the commitment to academic achievement is unwavering. The academic standing of incoming Northwestern football players is second among Division I-A schools only to Stanford's — a team in no danger of a Rose Bowl bid.

True, of the 71 players who've declared majors, 22 are enrolled in something called "Organizational Studies" — actually a watered-down business curriculum — and a few list majors like "Communication Studies" and "Psychological Services." But Northwestern proudly remains the only Big Ten school without the most abused jock-loophole of all, a school of education.

"There are definitely some athletic majors, but it's not like some schools where they study football," said Eric Chown, a former volunteer in the sports information office. "You see (linebacker) Pat Fitzgerald speaking so eloquently on TV, and you can't help but think, If that's what people think Northwestern students are like, that's fine with me."

In short, at Northwestern some things have changed, and some things will stay the same. But absolutely no one thinks the magic of this season will ever be duplicated — no matter what the team does in years to come.

Chown said: "I grew up a huge Michigan fan and went to all the games, even the Final Fours — but nothing, nothing Michigan has ever done has been even close to how good I feel about this team. Michigan's Fab Five beating Kentucky in overtime, that was great, but this season has been like that every week."

"It's been just a miracle kind of season," said Ken Kraft, the associate athletic director, who has seen enough Wildcat campaigns to know. "Even if you make two holes-in-one, the second one's not as much fun."

That Championship Season

Nemeth's Sweet Smell of Roses
The Wildcats' 1949 Trip to Pasadena Remembered

By Steve Kirk
Birmingham Post-Herald

BIRMINGHAM, Ala., Dec. 13, 1995 — A roomful of cynical old fellows stared at Gary Barnett in disbelief.

"We'll soon be in the Rose Bowl," Barnett said.

What? Had the Northwestern University football coach really just said that?

Two years ago, Ed Nemeth heard him say it. Nemeth had traveled from Birmingham to Evanston, Ill., to attend one of his 1949 Rose Bowl champion Wildcats football reunions, and he was part of the gathering of ex-jocks in the 60-something crowd at dinner that night.

And, no, he did not believe.

"He told us they were building and turning the corner," said Nemeth, now 70, who has watched his alma mater suffer miserably on the field the past 47 years. After all, the Wildcats' record between 1978 and 1994 was 32-151-4 so who could blame his reaction?

"We all said, 'Oh, yeah,'" Nemeth said.

To understand Northwestern's history is to understand the grins on the faces of its proud alumni this season as the team prepares for its second bowl game since it began playing football in 1882.

Just consider the time that's passed.

In post-World War II America, Nemeth — fresh off a three-year stay in Europe as a member of the 101st Airborne Combat Division — was a 5-foot-9, 192-pound left guard for the Wildcats.

"He was a little fireplug, short and stocky," said Dic Eggers, the '48 team's starting tackle and Nemeth's roommate and fraternity brother, "but, boy, could he carry his weight."

In post-George Bush America, Nemeth — fresh off retirement from a lifelong career in steel business management — is enjoying his new life as a grandfather in Vestavia Hills.

And, by the way, he now believes Barnett.

"By George," Nemeth said after watching the 1995 Wildcats run up a 10-1 record, a No. 3 ranking and a date with Southern Cal in the Jan. 1 Rose Bowl, "they kept winning."

Barnett knew what he was talking about after all. And because of that, Nemeth and his college buddies are packing their bags and taking their wives to Pasadena, Calif., for a New Year's party to celebrate.

When Ed and Nan Nemeth, who have lived in Birmingham since 1974, get to California, they'll hook up with old friends, old NU grads such as Steve Sawle, a starting tackle in '48 who lives in Lincolnshire, Ill., and his wife, Audrey.

Steve, the '49 team captain who lined up next to Nemeth on offense, loves to brag on "Hunky." Everyone had a nickname back then, and "Hunky" was Nemeth's. It referred to his stocky build.

"Hunky made up for his size with his aggressiveness." Steve said. Audrey is typical of Northwestern alumni, proud of the school but understanding of the football team's fate.

"Several years ago," Audrey said, "I gave my husband a trip to the Rose Bowl when Iowa played. Because I said, 'Well, Northwestern will never go, and I want you to see the Rose Bowl.

You played in the Rose Bowl, but I want you to see the Rose Bowl.'"

The Sawles will be back at this season's Rose Bowl.

"A lot of people see Northwestern as an underdog story that can win," Audrey said. "Hey, put that across your life. People see an underdog can win. I really think there's a great message there."

The message is not lost on Nemeth, who said, "I am very proud," as his scrapbook of the '49 Rose Bowl sits nearby.

Nemeth actually started school at the University of Illinois, and played three games for the Fighting Illini in the fall of 1943 before the military called and he was sent to the war.

When he returned to the states, the GI Bill helped Nemeth return to school — and his good grades at Washington High in his hometown of East Chicago,

Ind., helped him get accepted at Northwestern, still today better known for its academics than its athletics.

Coach Lynn "Pappy" Waldorf left after Nemeth's first season in '46 and Bob Voigts took over the program. Ironically it was Waldorf's California team that Northwestern defeated, 20-14, in the '49 Rose Bowl during Nemeth's junior season, the team's only winning season during Nemeth's four years in Evanston.

The Wildcats, who had a 7-2 regular-season record that year, actually finished second in the Big Ten, but they got the Rose Bowl trip because the rule then was that a team couldn't make consecutive appearances in the Rose Bowl. Conference champion Michigan had gone the year before.

Sure, that trip to Southern California was fun. Nemeth remembers riding the Super Chief train of the Santa Fe line, meeting Bob Hope and touring Paramount Studios. But the trip, on which Nan — a Pasadena native — accompanied the team along with one other coed and several faculty members, was about winning, too.

"It was exciting for them," said Nan, who graduated in 1952, two years after Ed graduated and one year before they married.

"What I remember most is that there was some feeling from the Pac 10 that they really shouldn't be playing Northwestern, because Michigan had won the Big Ten title. So it was really important to beat them."

And win they did. Trailing with less than two min-

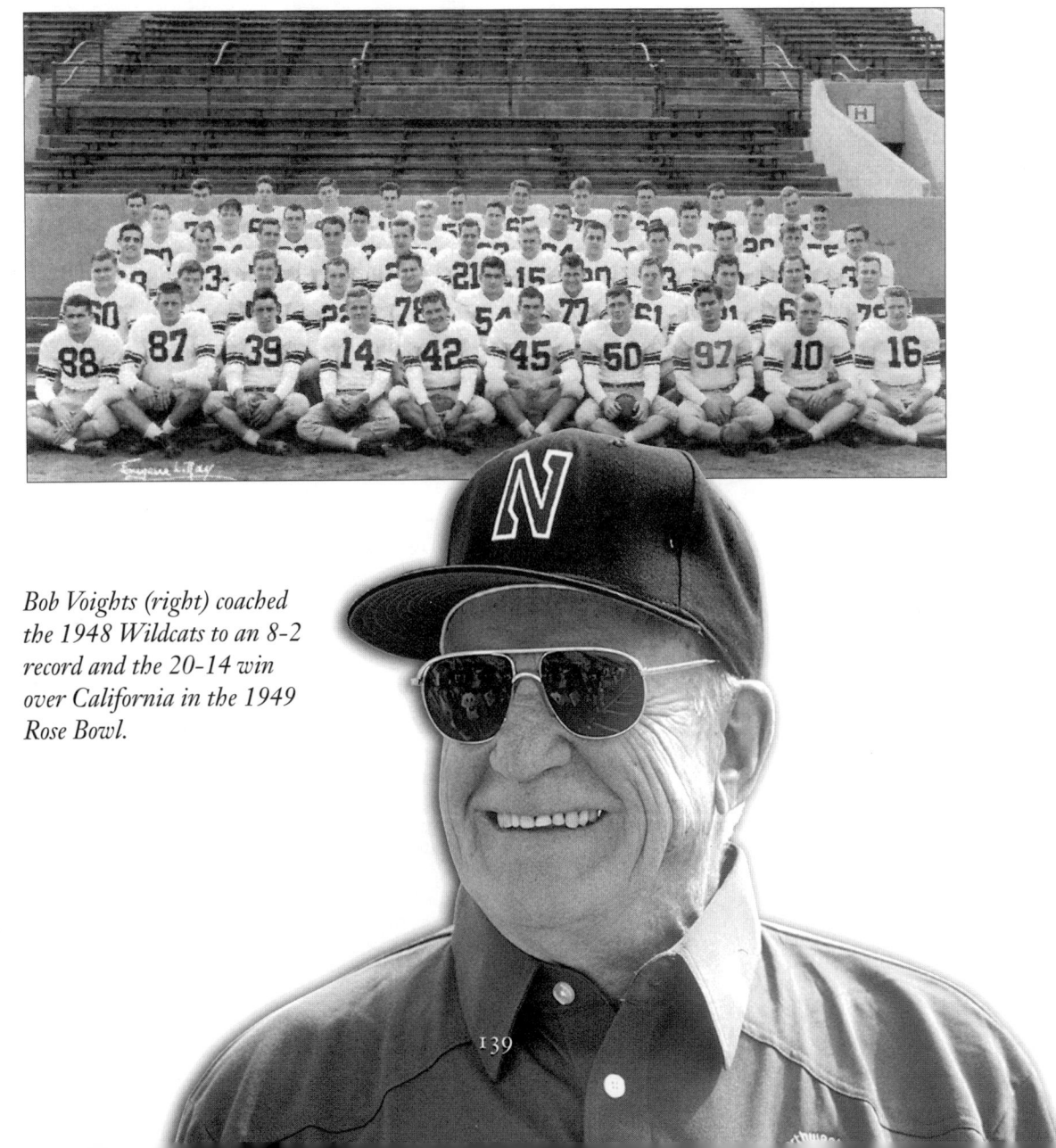

Bob Voights (right) coached the 1948 Wildcats to an 8-2 record and the 20-14 win over California in the 1949 Rose Bowl.

utes to play, Voigts called for a trick play in front of more than 90,000 fans. Instead of snapping the ball to the quarterback in Northwestern's T-formation, center Alex Sarkisian snapped it to right halfback Ed Tunnicliff, who held the ball behind his back while all-America fullback Art Murakowski took off to the left, along with the quarterback and left halfback, and drew the defense with him. That's when Tunnicliff ran to the right and scored a touchdown 43 yards later.

"It worked beautifully," said Nemeth, who was presented a videotape of the game at a recent reunion. "We fooled the California team."

And when it was over, Waldorf went to the Northwestern dressing room to congratulate his former players.

"Boys, I felt today I couldn't lose," he said to a roomful of tears.

Murakowski since has died, but many members of the team will be in Pasadena on New Year's Day. So far, 26 members of the team have confirmed reservations for the trip, Nan said.

The Nemeths plan to stay with their daughter Sally, a television and film writer in Hollywood.

And, as they have done several times this year in Alabama, they plan to brag on their alma mater. "When Northwestern had won a couple of games (earlier this season and Alabama and Auburn had lost a couple of games), I had fun with my friends," Nemeth said. "But Northwestern's kind of the country's favorite."

Ed Nemeth played on Northwestern's 1949 Rose Bowl team.

And folks everywhere, from Northwestern graduates such as Charleton Heston and Brent Musburger to that roomful of ex-jocks, believe.

Notre Dame's Lancaster Smith pulls down Art Murakowski in the 1948 Notre Dame-NU contest, which was won by the Irish, 12-7.

Chapter 15

A Knight on the Field

Darnell Autry Leads NU to Greatness

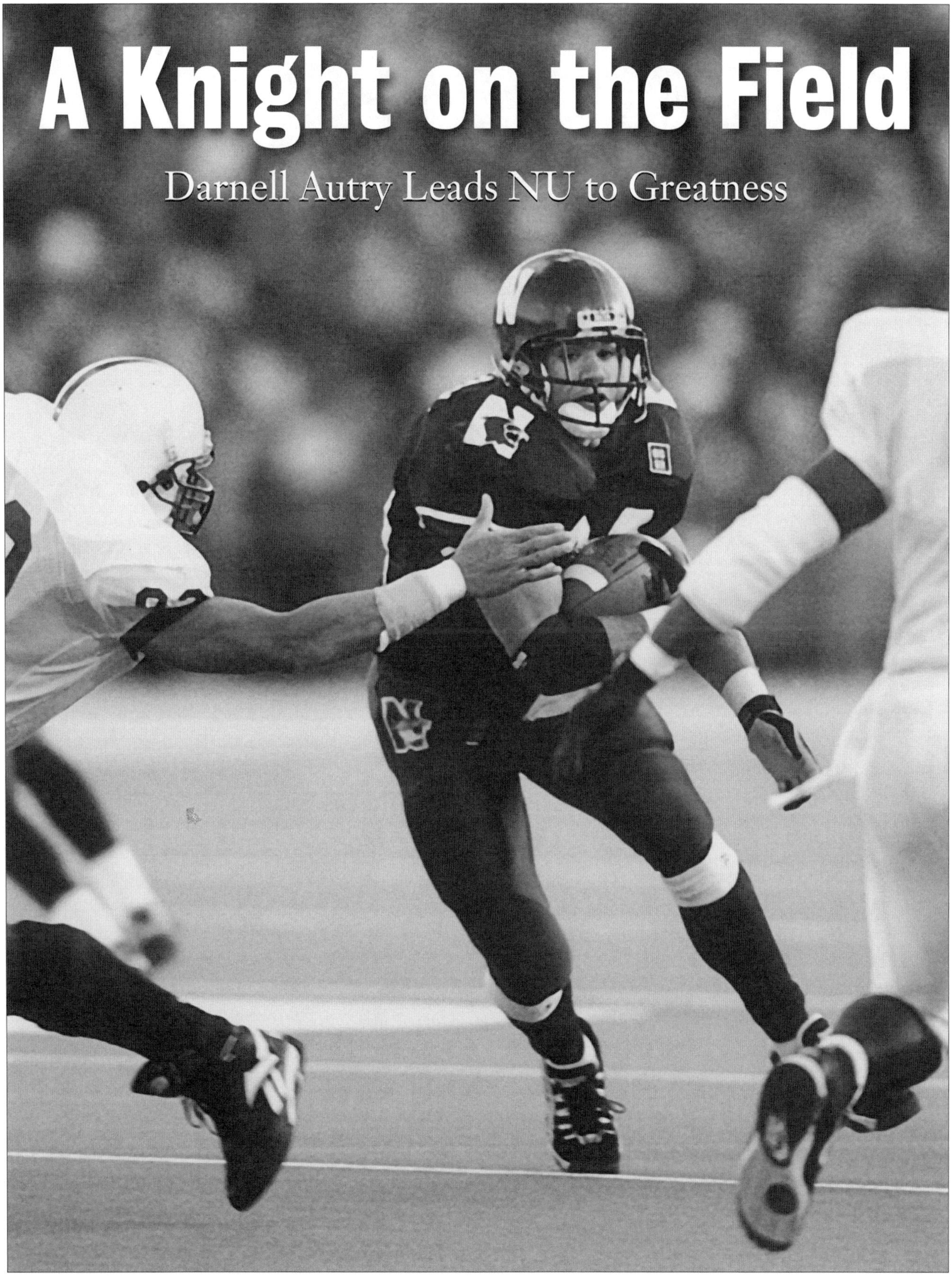

141

That Championship Season

By Francis J. Fitzgerald

WASHINGTON, Dec. 15, 1995 — He is the ultimate college running back. A cross between Emmitt Smith and Tony Dorsett. And he is one of the biggest factors in Northwestern's meteoric rise to the top of the college football world in 1995.

Darnell Autry, a 6-foot-1, 211 lb. sophomore halfback, broke all of the Northwestern rushing records as the Wildcats performed their storybook miracle this fall. At the end of the 1995 season, Autry had rushed for a school-record 1,675 yards. He also set school records for carries (350), points (90), touchdowns (15) and rushing TD's (14) in a single season and was fifth in the nation and second in the Big Ten in rushing and 12th nationally in scoring. Autry averaged 4.7 yards per carry and continued his 12-game streak of 100-yard games.

At Tempe, Ariz., High School, Autry scored 19 touchdowns in his senior season and averaged 9.8 yards per carry. Off the field, he set Arizona schoolboy records in the 100- and 200-meter dashes in the state track and field meet.

West Coast heavyweights U.C.L.A., Arizona State and Colorado and the Big East Syracuse recruited him to play in the secondary. But Autry chose Northwestern because of its renowned drama program and the opportunity to play in the offensive backfield.

As a freshman for the Wildcats in 1994, Autry rushed for 556 yards on 120 attempts for a 4.6-yard average, had a pair of 100-yard games and started in Northwestern's final contest against Penn State.

Following the season, however, Autry got a case of homesickness and had to be convinced by Wildcats' coach Gary Barnett and fellow teammates to stay at the Evanston campus.

"My dad was hot that I wanted to leave," Autry later explained. "It had nothing to do with here (at NU). He thought I'd be throwing away all that I had. He told me to grow up and be a man."

Eventually, the homesickness was cured and Autry joined his teammates in spring practice and began to put together the Northwestern Miracle that has since enchanted an entire country.

In November, Autry graced the front cover of *Sports Illustrated* and was picked as a finalist in the voting for the Heisman Trophy. Little of this adulation, however, has effected NU's newest hero.

"This season has been a dream," he explained to sportswriters at the end of the regular season. "We have chemistry. We're of different races and from different places, but on the field we are all the same. It's tough to find a team like that."

With a Big Ten title and a Rose Bowl bid now safely tucked away, Autry and his Northwestern teammates have proven to be more than 1995's team of destiny.

They have been an example to all of us, proving that with a lot of hard work dreams really do come true.

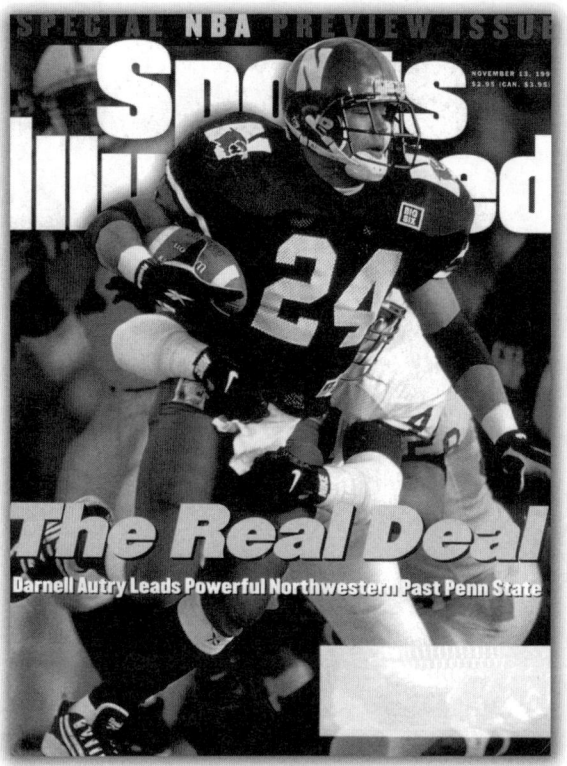

THE STREAK

Northwestern's Darnell Autry is the only running back in Division I-A to have more than 100 yards in every game:

Opponent	Rush	Yards	TD
Notre Dame	33	160	0
Miami (Ohio)	35	152	0
Air Force	37	190	2
Indiana	28	162	2
Michigan	26	103	0
Minnesota	28	169	3
Wisconsin*	27	113	2
Illinois	41	151	1
Penn State	36	139	3
Iowa	32	110	1
Purdue	32	226	0
TOTALS	355	1,675	14

*Autry's original 81-yard performance against Wisconsin was later revised to give him a total of 113 yards rushing.

Darnell Autry: First team All-Big Ten, second team all-America and No. 4 in the Heisman Trophy balloting.

After Ryan Padgett clears a hole in the Wisconsin line, Autry runs for daylight. He would eventually score 2 touchdowns against the Badgers.

Autry Finishes 4th in Heisman Balloting

By Rick Warner
The Associated Press

NEW YORK, Dec. 9, 1995 — Eddie George, who led the nation with 24 touchdowns and rushed for an Ohio State-record 1,826 yards, won the Heisman Trophy Saturday evening.

George, a senior tailback, beat out Nebraska's Tommie Frazier and Florida's Danny Wuerffel, the quarterback on the top two teams in the country, by a wide margin.

Darnell Autry, the sophomore Northwestern halfback who led the Wildcats in the greatest turnaround in college football history and a Rose Bowl berth against U.S.C. on New Year's Day, finished fourth in the balloting.

After hearing the announcement, George buried his head in his hands.

"I'm glad this is over," he said. "I'm just overwhelmed right now."

The announcement came two weeks after Ohio State's perfect season and national championship hopes were dashed by a 31-23 loss to Michigan which gave the Big Ten title and Rose Bowl bid to Northwestern.

The Heisman vote

Player	School	Points
Eddie George	Ohio State	1,460
Tommie Frazier	Nebraska	1,196
Danny Wuerffel	Florida	987
Darnell Autry	Northwestern	535
Troy Davis	Iowa State	402

CHAPTER 16

The Purple to Pasadena

In Rose Bowl, The Clock Strikes Midnight for Cats

That Championship Season

By Steve Wilstein
The Associated Press

PASADENA, Calif., Jan. 1, 1996 — Maybe it was too much to ask, too farfetched that purple-clad Northwestern players could stroll into the Rose Bowl for the first time since 1949 and beat Southern California practically on its own turf.

Well, the improbable nearly happened in a game that came close to a football fantasy.

Two painful mistakes aside, nothing Northwestern did in the Rose Bowl marred its amazing transformation from chump to Big Ten champ.

Third-ranked Northwestern put on a memorable show in its first bowl game since 1949, only to lose to a Southern Cal that salvaged a season of bitter losses with a 41-32 victory.

No. 17 Southern California didn't get suckered by Northwestern's mystique or ground down by the Wildcats' running game and 300-pound linemen.

Instead, the Trojans cranked up their passing attack and stiffened their defense, scoring on a 53-yard fumble return by Daylon McCutcheon and securing victory with an interception by Jesse Davis in the final minutes.

Those two turnovers, uncharacteristic of Northwestern this season, made all the difference in a game that saw a Rose Bowl record performance by U.S.C. all-America receiver Keyshawn Johnson, who had 12 catches for 216 yards and a TD.

"This was a great football game, and our guys deserved it," said U.S.C. coach John Robinson, who

With a packed house of 100,000-plus at the Rose Bowl — one-third of these were Northwestern fans — the Purple returned to Pasadena for the first time since 1949.

Southern Cal 41
Northwestern 32

Southern Cal	7	17	7	10-41
Northwestern	7	3	16	6-32

USC: L.Woods 1-yard run (Abrams kick)
NU: D.Autry 3-yard run (Gowins kick)
USC: Barnum 21-yard pass from Otton (Abrams kick)
USC: FG Abrams 30 yards
USC: McCutcheon 53-yard fumble return (Abrams kick)
NU: FG Gowins 29 yards
NU: FG Gowins 28 yards
NU: D.Autry 9-yard run (pass failed)
USC: K.Johnson 56-yard pass from Otton (Abrams kick)
NU: Schnur 1-yard run (Gowins kick)
NU: D.Autry 2-yard run (run failed)
USC: FG Abrams 46 yards
USC: Washington 2-yard run (Abrams kick)
A: 100,102

	USC	NU
First downs	22	23
Rushes-yards	27-33	39-139
Passing	391	336
Return yards	59	0
Comp-att-int	29-44-0	23-39-1
Punts	2-45	2-39
Fumbles-lost	1-1	1-1
Penalties-yards	11-86	7-72
Time of possession	29:47	30:13

RUSHING: Southern Cal, Washington 16-51, Barnum 1-2, L.Woods 5-2, Otton 5-(minus 22). Northwestern, D.Autry 32-110, Schnur 3-13, A.Autry 2-8, Bates 1-4, Hartl 1-4.
PASSING: Southern Cal, Otton 29-44-0-391. Northwestern, Schnur 23-39-1-336.
RECEIVING: Southern Cal, K.Johnson 12-216, Barnum 4-42, C.Miller 3-50, Cashman 3-19, L.Woods 2-21, McWilliams 2-20, Washington 2-18, Parker 1-5. Northwestern, Bates 7-145, D.Autry 6-38, Musso 5-91, Beazley 1-16, Drexler 1-16, McGrew 1-11, Hartl 1-10, Brown 1-9.

Road to the Rose Bowl

After trailing, 24-10, at halftime, Darnell Autry – who scored three touchdowns and rushed for 110 yards – led the Wildcats in a 22-point second-half scoring spree and captured the lead, 32-31, early in the fourth quarter.

was beleaguered by criticism on campus after losses to longtime rivals Notre Dame and U.C.L.A.

"We knew going in we were definitely the straight men, but not now. We wanted to come out and take the initiative, but they did a great job of coming back."

Brad Otton, who usually alternates at quarterback with Kyle Wachholtz, played the whole game, keeping the Trojans moving and completing 29 of 44 for 391 yards and two touchdowns.

"I went to coach Robby," Johnson said, "and I said, 'Let me and Brad take care of things.' Once I realized Kyle wasn't going, it was time for me to jump on the bandwagon with Brad."

Johnson, who was named the game's MVP, broke the 176-yard receiving record set last year by U.C.L.A.'s J.J. Stokes.

Steve Schnur completed 23 of 38 passes for 336 yards for the Wildcats, including 145 yards to D'Wayne Bates.

Darnell Autry carried 32 times for 110 yards and three touchdowns. It was the 13th straight game in which he has rushed for more than 100 yards.

Otton opened the game with a 13-yard pass to

NU's third quarter blitz gave Wildcats fans back at The Huddle in Evanston a lot to cheer about. But U.S.C. receiver Keyshawn Johnson (3) single-handedly quieted the Rose Bowl crowd in the fourth quarter.

ROAD TO THE ROSE BOWL

That Championship Season

U.S.C.'s potent passing offense and a pair of rare NU errors at crucial moments in the game gave Wildcats coach Gary Barnett much to worry about.

LaVale Woods, kept finding receivers down to the 1 with a surprising no-huddle offense, then handed off to Woods for a touchdown leap to cap an 83-yard drive.

Northwestern (10-2) came back to tie the game on a 68-yard drive that ended with Autry bulling in for a touchdown from 3 yards out.

U.S.C. (9-2-1) made it 14-7 early in the second quarter when Johnson caught three straight passes for 46 yards, and Otton found fullback Terry Barnum in the corner of the end zone for a 21-yard TD.

Johnson expressed resentment at all the attention directed toward Northwestern, whose purple-clad fans made up nearly a third of the 100,102 in attendance at the Rose Bowl.

"They wanted purple this and purple that," Johnson said. "They had it until midnight, and then their dream was over."

After Northwestern's replacement kicker Brian Gowins missed a 37-yard field goal attempt, U.S.C. made it 17-7 on Adam Abrams' 30-yard field goal.

Northwestern, which thrived this year by scoring on other teams' turnovers, lost the ball with 2:56 left in the half when Brian Musso fumbled trying to get more yards on a pass across the middle. It was the 13th turnover in 12 games for Northwestern, which forced its opponents to commit 32 turnovers. McCutcheon picked up the ball and ran down the sideline for the score and a 24-7 U.S.C. lead.

"No one gave us any respect," McCutcheon said, "and I think it got some of the players down, and some of the players fired up. We were ready to play this game, and we just wanted to end all that mess.

"We're tired of hearing about Northwestern. Everyone thought Northwestern was going to win this game, and we had a lot to prove — especially after that U.C.L.A. loss."

Northwestern coach Gary Barnett rued his team's mistakes.

"When you turn the ball over, you're playing against two forces — yourselves and U.S.C.," Barnett said. "We turned the ball over twice, and we haven't done that all year. People have committed those errors against us, and we took advantage of them. You're not going to win bowl games playing this caliber of football."

150

A fumble by Woods on U.S.C.'s 34 with 12 seconds left in the half led to a 29-yard field goal by Gowins that cut the deficit to 24-10.

Northwestern chipped away at U.S.C. with an 18-yard field goal on the opening drive of the second half to make it 24-13, then caught U.S.C. by surprise with an onside kick the Wildcats recovered on their 48.

The Wildcats scored quickly on Autry's 9-yard run. A two-point conversion pass failed, but suddenly the Wildcats were back in contention at 24-19 with 8:17 left in the third quarter.

That shift of momentum changed two minutes later when Otton drilled a pass over the middle to Johnson, two steps ahead of the nearest defender around Northwestern's 40, and watched Johnson race untouched for a 56-yard touchdown and a 31-19 U.S.C. lead.

Northwestern, which came from behind to win four games during the regular season, came back again with another surprise. Schnur faked an end-around and threw a 46-yard pass that Bates leaped for and caught between two defenders on the U.S.C. 26. Five plays later Schnur sneaked over the goal line on a 1-yard run that cut the lead to 31-26.

After Northwestern's defense forced the Trojans to punt from their own 7, Autry completed a 57-yard drive with a 2-yard TD scamper that put the Wildcats ahead for the first time, 32-31, with 13:01 left in the game.

A 46-yard field goal by Abrams four minutes later put the Trojans back on top, 34-32.

The Wildcats appeared to be driving toward another score with 6:42 left when a second huge turnover stopped them — the interception by Davis, who returned the ball 39 yards to Northwestern's 31. That led to a 2-yard TD leap by Delon Washington that put U.S.C. safely ahead, 41-32, with 2:55 left.

The Rose Bowl championship went a long way toward dimming the memory of U.S.C.'s losses to its archrivals and should take some of the heat off John Robinson.

Forty-seven years after its only other bowl game, a Rose Bowl victory, Northwestern sought to put the last wonderful touch on one of college football's greatest and most improbable seasons.

Frustrated NU quarterback Steve Schnur reacts to a second-half interception.

That Championship Season

The purple-clad Wildcats, pushed around like 98-pound weaklings by their Big Ten brethren for years, humbled traditional powerhouses Notre Dame, Michigan and Penn State, but couldn't quite catch up to U.S.C.

Yet this Northwestern team, coming off 3-7 and 2-9 seasons the last two years, could feel nothing but pride in the way it played right to the end. Northwestern hadn't had a winning season since 1971 — before any of the current players were born — and on this day it came close to winning the Rose Bowl.

So close, that Barnett didn't hesitate about the chances of coming back.

"We have proven," he said, "that when we can play together and recreate the chemistry we had this year, anything's possible."

(Left) Wildcats lineman Don Holmes attempts to sack U.S.C. quarterback Brad Otten. Otten would connect on 29 of 44 passes and two touchdowns against NU. (Above) In the first quarter, Trojan tailback LaVale Woods dives over the top for a touchdown against Northwestern.

That Championship Season

A Journey and a Dream Fall Short
U.S.C. Launches Aerial Attack to Stop Cats' Bandwagon

By Rick Gano
The Associated Press

PASADENA, Calif., Jan. 1, 1996 — The purple-clad season that captivated college football didn't come up rosy for Northwestern's Wildcats. Winning the Rose Bowl was beyond their reach.

"It's not what it could have been. But I don't know if it's tainted," NU coach Gary Barnett said minutes after a tough 41-32 loss to Southern California.

"We came from nowhere and we did some good things. We didn't win the Rose Bowl. Now we have to come back and win it."

The Wildcats, in their first bowl appearance in 47

A Championship Season to Remember

It started with a shocking upset at Notre Dame and ended with a Big Ten title and a trip to the Rose Bowl. A look at Northwestern's improbable season, and how the team was ranked weekly by The Associated Press:

Key
Wildcats' national ranking after each game.
N= Not ranked

	Sept. 2	Sept. 16	Sept. 23	Sept. 30	Oct. 7
Ranking	N	N	N	25	14
Score	Northwestern 17 / Notre Dame 15	Miami (Ohio) 30 / Northwestern 28	Northwestern 30 / Air Force 6	Northwestern 31 / Indiana 6	Northwestern 19 / Michigan 13
Opponent	Notre Dame	Miami (Ohio)	Air Force	Indiana	Michigan
Notes	The impossible dream begins; the Wildcats and Darnell Autry stun the Irish and the nation.	The Wildcats suffer their only setback, blowing the game on a botched punt snap.	Rebound time: Northwestern looks impressive shutting down the Falcons.	The voters finally take notice, as the Wildcats trounce the Hoosiers.	The Wildcats show they are for real. The defense, led by Pat Fitzgerald, stops the Wolverines.

ROAD TO THE ROSE BOWL

years, fell behind 24-7, took the lead with a colossal second-half rally, and then succumbed to the speed and passing game of the Trojans.

Not since the 1949 Rose Bowl, a 20-14 victory over California, had Northwestern played in a postseason game. The interim was filled with long bouts of losing and jokes about their futility. Until this year, the Wildcats had not had a winning season since 1971.

There were long faces but no tears when the Wildcats emerged from their locker room.

"Of course the goal is to win the Rose Bowl; that's what the goal has to be every year," said senior center Rob Johnson, who withstood the lean times. "But to change a program the way we did this year is something to behold. It's something that will still be written about 30 or 40 or 50 years from now."

Even though the bowl experience was a first for the Northwestern players, jitters didn't beat the Wildcats. Southern Cal's passing game did. The Trojans' combination of Brad Otton to Keyshawn Johnson was unlike any other the Wildcats had faced this year, even as they went 10-1 and beat Notre Dame, Michigan and Penn State in a season no could have imagined.

"Otton and Keyshawn were just a little above every-

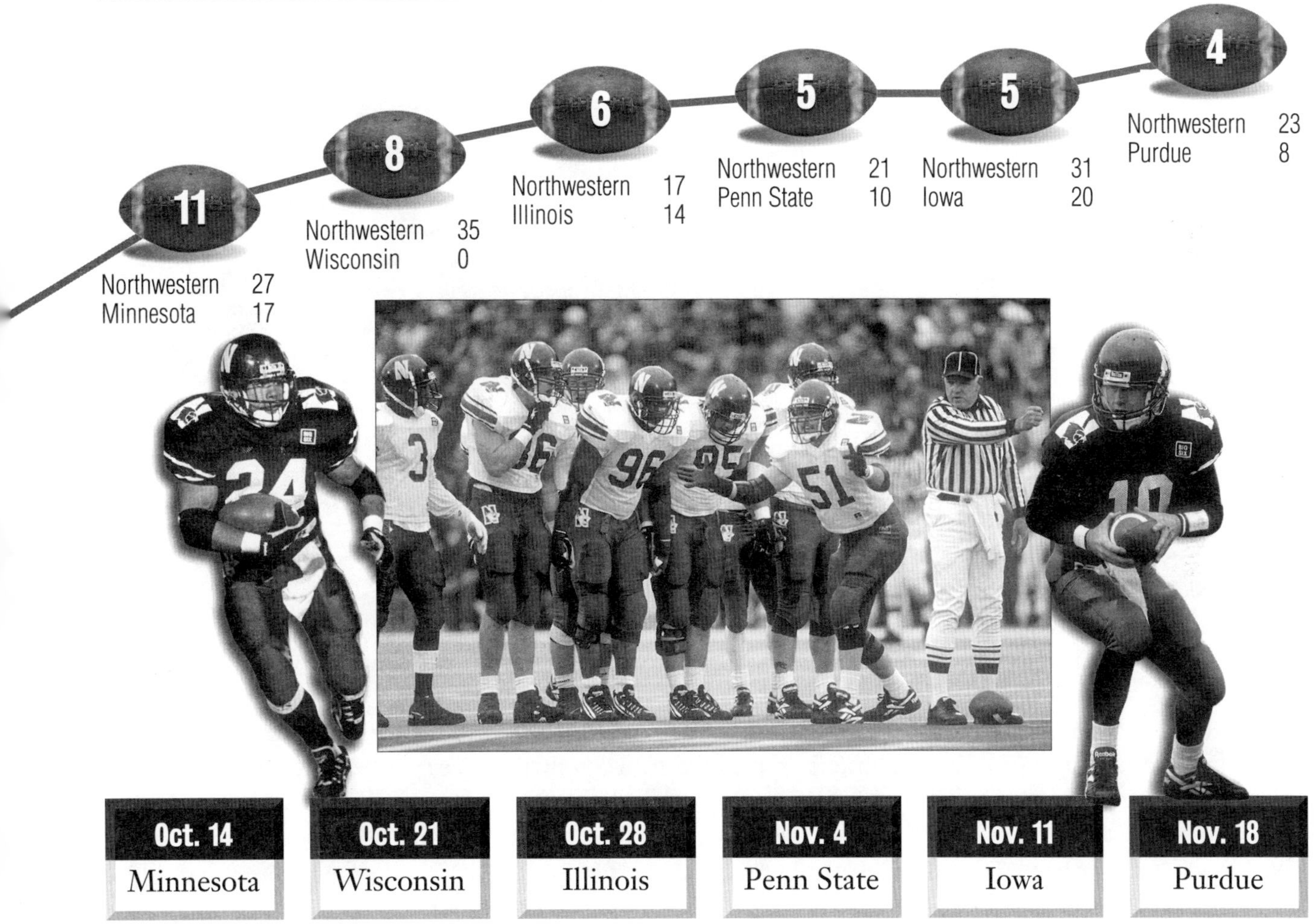

	11	8	6	5	5	4
	Northwestern 27 Minnesota 17	Northwestern 35 Wisconsin 0	Northwestern 17 Illinois 14	Northwestern 21 Penn State 10	Northwestern 31 Iowa 20	Northwestern 23 Purdue 8

Oct. 14	Oct. 21	Oct. 28	Nov. 4	Nov. 11	Nov. 18
Minnesota	Wisconsin	Illinois	Penn State	Iowa	Purdue
The Wildcats trail early, but the Autry Express takes over in the second half.	Wildcat fever takes over Evanson after the Wildcats' most impressive victory of the year.	Illinois jumps to a 14-0 lead, but the Wildcats win on Autry's fourth-quarter touchdown.	The Wildcats make a believer out of Joe Paterno with a convincing victory.	The Wildcats take command in the second half to defeat the Hawkeyes for the first time since 1973.	Wildcats clinch share of Big Ten title. A week later, Michigan's defeat of Ohio State gives NU a Rose Bowl berth.

body else on the field. Even when we knew they were going to throw the ball to him, we couldn't put enough pressure on the quarterback or cover Keyshawn well enough," said Barnett, who has been linked the last week to the coaching vacancy at U.C.L.A.

Otton completed 29 of 44 passes for 391 yards, and Johnson made 12 catches for 216 yards.

The Wildcats also made two uncharacteristic mistakes. They'd forced 32 turnovers during the season and committed just 12.

Southern California's Daylon McCutcheon scooped up a fumble by Brian Musso after a pass reception and ran 53 yards for a touchdown to help the Trojans build their big lead. Southern Cal then ensured the victory when Jesse Davis picked off Steve Schnur in the fourth quarter.

"We feel bad right now. But there is a lot we did this year. Looking back on it none of us dreamed of being in this situation," said Schnur, who threw 39 times, after averaging 19 passes a game during the season.

"I wish I could go back and change some things that happened today and we could win the game but you can't," Schnur said. "That's why there's next year."

Musso thought his knee was down before the fumble, a play that put U.S.C. ahead, 24-7.

"It happened so fast, it's hard to say," Musso said. "The refs called it like they see it. And I can't change it, I got to live with it. The game is not going to change.

"We can never duplicate a season like this. Hopefully we'll never be 3-7-1 again and we'll never again be in the doghouse of the Big Ten. The surprise of this season to a lot of people is kind of what captured the nation.

"In a sense, we can't duplicate it. But getting back to the Rose Bowl ... we can duplicate that."

Northwestern, buoyed by a sea of followers donned in purple, white and black among the 100,102 in this majestic stadium, kept coming back. Finally, on Darnell Autry's third touchdown run, the Wildcats had the lead at 32-31 in the final quarter.

But this story didn't end like so many others.

Southern Cal got a late field goal, and then the inter-

BROKEN DREAMS: *A dejected Rodney Ray, the NU defensive back, reflects on a memorable 1995 season and a Rose Bowl game the Wildcats almost won.*

ception by Davis preceded a clinching touchdown by Delon Washington with just over three minutes left.

Northwestern entered the game with a defense that allowed only 12.7 points a game — the best in the nation. But they had trouble pressuring Otton, and the dream was finally over for a school long known more for its academics than athletics.

"I'll walk away from this place saying, 'What if?' for the rest of my life," linebacker Geoff Shein said. "That is a horrible feeling to have."

1995 Northwestern Wildcats Roster

No.	Name	Pos.	Ht.	Wt.	Class	Hometown (High School/JC)
9	Abramson, Lloyd	QB	6-3	218	So.	Bloomfield, Mich. (Seaholm)
48	Allen, Eugene	DB	5-10	193	So.	Indianapolis, Ind. (Lawrence Central)
32	Autry, Adrian	RB	5-11	185	So.	Long Grove, Ill. (Loyola Academy)
24	Autry, Darnell*	RB	6-1	211	So.	Tempe, Ariz. (Tempe)
17	Barnes, Josh	DB	5-11	170	So.	Cleveland, Ohio (Case Western Reserve Prep)
5	Bates, D'Wayne	WR	6-3	195	So.	Aiken, S.C. (Silver Bluff)
86	Beazley, Dave	WR	5-9	185	Sr.	Crystal Lake, Ill. (Central)
20	Bennett, William	FS	6-1	190	Sr.	Tempe, Ariz. (Marcos de Niza)
34	Brown, Levelle	RB	6-0	208	Fr.	Naperville, Ill. (North)
71	Brownstein, Bo	OL	6-6	260	Fr.	Englewood, Colo. (Kent Denver)
12	Broxtermann, Mark	QB	5-11	160	Fr.	Homewood, Ill. (Marian Catholic)
49	Buck, Kevin	OLB	6-3	205	Fr.	Miami, Fla. (Killian)
80	Burden, John	WR	6-4	193	So.	Orlando, Fla. (Boone)
81	Burns, Jon	DT	6-6	270	So.	Kankakee, Ill. (Bishop McNamara)
7	Burrell, Aaron	RB	6-2	190	Fr.	Cedar Rapids, Iowa (Washington)
14	Burton, Paul	P	5-11	185	Sr.	Framingham, Mass. (Framingham)
47	Campbell, Morgan	CB	5-7	160	Fr.	Ontario, Canada (The Woodlands School)
61	Chabot, Justin	OT	6-6	285	Sr.	Oxford, Ohio (Talawanda)
33	Collier, Eric	SS	6-2	215	Jr.	Dixon, Ill. (Dixon)
11	Conoway, Gerald	DB	6-1	175	Fr.	Detroit, Mich. (Detroit Country Day)
89	Curry, Larry	DT	6-4	273	Sr.	Granite City, Ill. (Granite City)
36	Dailey, Casey	OLB	6-4	242	Jr.	La Verne, Calif. (Damien)
2	Davis, Mike	WR	6-4	210	Fr.	San Diego, Calif. (Grossmont)
76	Dodge, Tony	OL	6-6	310	Fr.	McHenry, Ill. (McHenry)
83	Drexler, Darren	TE	6-6	260	Sr.	Kirkwood, Mo. (Kirkwood)
88	DuBose, KeJaun	DT	6-3	273	Jr.	Jennings, Mo. (Jennings)
65	Dyra, Jeff	DL	6-4	245	Fr.	Chicago, Ill. (St. Patrick)
51	Fitzgerald, Pat	ILB	6-4	228	Jr.	Orland Park, Ill. (Carl Sandburg)
35	Fordenwalt, Matt	TE	6-3	227	Fr.	Seville, Ohio (Cloverleaf)
99	Friedrich, Ryan	DL	6-8	270	Fr.	Stevens Point, Wis. (Stevens Point)
55	Gardner, Barry	LB	5-11	232	So.	Harvey, Ill. (Thorton)
43	Gaston, Stafford	LB	6-3	230	Fr.	Oklahoma City, Okla. (Northeast)
92	Giometti, Mike	DL	6-3	234	Sr.	Lake Forest, Ill. (Lake Forest)
66	Gnos, Graham	OL	6-3	276	Sr.	Bloomington, Minn. (Jefferson)
38	Gooch, Tyrone	RB	5-11	175	Fr.	Bolingbrook, Ill. (Waubonsie Valley)
13	Gowins, Brian	PK	5-9	160	So.	Birmingham, Ala. (Shades Valley)
84	Graham, Shane	TE	6-6	260	Sr.	Thousand Oaks, Calif. (Thousand Oaks)
1	Guess, Larry	WR	6-3	190	Jr.	Hinsdale, Ill. (South)
4	Hamdorf, Chris	QB	6-3	196	Jr.	Iowa City, Iowa (Iowa City)
85	Harpring, Brian	TE	6-3	267	Sr.(5)	Dunwoody, Ga. (Atlanta Marist)
46	Hartl, Matt	FB	6-3	225	So.	Denver, Colo. (Washington)
70	Hemmerle, Brian	OT	6-7	270	Fr.	Louisville, Ky. (Trinity)
41	Henkelmann, Matt	WR	6-2	177	So.	Linton, N.D. (Linton)
53	Holmes, Don	LB	6-0	240	So.	South Holland, Ill. (Thornwood)
8	Hughes, Tim	QB	6-3	215	Jr.	Gridley, Calif. (Gridley/Butte Comm. College)
74	Janus, Paul	OL	6-5	278	Jr.	Edgerton, Wis. (Edgerton)
57	Johnson, Rob	C	6-4	270	Sr.(5)	Chicago, Ill. (St. Francis de Sales)
39	Jones, Shannon	PK	5-9	190	So.	Grand Rapids, Mich. (East Grand Rapids)
78	Kardos, Brian	OT	6-5	285	Sr.	Springfield, Ill. (Sacred Heart-Griffin)

No.	Name	Pos.	Ht.	Wt.	Class	Hometown (High School/JC)
40	Kolar, Josh	LB	6-4	220	Fr.	Wilmette, Ill. (New Trier)
79	LaBelle, Bryan	OT	6-6	304	So.	Kent, Wash. (Kentwood)
91	Lapadula, Marc	LB	6-3	240	Fr.	Allentown, Pa. (Central Catholic)
37	Leary, Faraji	RB	6-1	205	So.	Buffalo Grove, Ill. (Stevenson)
69	Leeder, Chris	OL	6-4	292	So.	Rockford, Mich. (Rockford)
44	Lozowski, Keith	OLB	6-2	251	Jr.	Palatine, Ill. (Fremd)
28	MacLeod, Doug	DB/PK	5-11	195	So.	Wheaton, Ill. (Wheaton-Warrenville South)
16	Martin, Chris	CB	5-9	180	Sr.	Tampa, Fla. (Jesuit)
58	Matiyow, Jason	C	6-3	255	Fr.	Council Bluffs, Iowa (Lewis Central)
88	McCaffrey, James	TE	6-1	195	Fr.	Schaumburg, Ill. (Saint Viator)
45	McGrew, Mike	FB	6-0	216	Sr.	Chicago Heights, Ill. (Mt. Carmel)
89	McLain, Randy	OLB	6-3	200	Fr.	Isanti, Minn. (Saint Francis)
42	Morrison, Tucker	LB	6-2	225	Jr.	Seattle, Wash. (Orchard Park)
22	Musso, Brian	WR	6-0	186	Jr.	Hinsdale, Ill. (Central)
23	Musso, Scott	RB	5-11	195	Fr.	Hinsdale, Ill. (Central)
26	Nelson Jr., Mike	DB	6-2	200	So.	Plano, Texas (Plano East)
54	Offenbacher, Shawn	OL	6-1	270	So.	Chesterfield, Mo. (Parkway Central)
93	Oropeza, Luis	LB	6-1	226	Jr.	Red Bluff, Calif. (Butte Comm. College)
75	Padgett, Ryan	OG	6-3	285	Sr.	Bellevue, Wash. (Newport)
72	Peterson, Kevin	OG	6-4	282	Sr.	Lockport, Ill. (Lockport)
6	Price, Marcel	DB	6-1	190	So.	Nashville, Tenn. (Whites Creek)
77	Pugh, Chad	OG	6-3	279	Sr.	Oswego, Ill. (Oswego)
15	Ray, Rodney	CB	5-11	190	Sr.(5)	Ferguson, Mo. (Florrisant McCluer)
62	Reed, Adam	C	6-3	275	So.	Boulder, Colo. (Boulder)
94	Reiff, Joe	DT	6-4	270	Sr.	Cedar Rapids, Iowa (Prairie)
95	Rice, Matt	DT	6-3	255	Jr.	Middleton, Wis. (Middleton)
96	Robey, Ray	DT	6-4	270	Jr.	Rockford, Ill. (Auburn)
29	Rooney, Chris	CB	5-8	181	Sr.	Minneapolis, Minn. (Breck School)
59	Ross, Jason	LB	6-1	227	So.	Dayton, Ohio (Miamisburg)
19	Rubin, Brian	DB	5-9	175	Fr.	Detroit, Mich. (Detroit Country Day)
98	Russ, Bobby	DL	6-4	275	So.	Calumet City, Ill. (Thornton Fractional North)
31	Sanders, Kyle	OLB	6-0	195	Fr.	Jackson, Mich. (Jackson)
52	Scharf, Tim	ILB	6-2	240	Jr.	Rockford, Ill. (Boylan Central Catholic)
90	Schmidt, Thor	OLB	6-3	240	So.	Santa Barbara, Calif. (Bishop Garcia Diego)
10	Schnur, Steve	QB	6-1	190	Sr.	St. Louis, Mo. (St. Louis University)
47	Shein, Geoff	OLB	6-2	224	Sr.(5)	Glencoe, Ill. (Deerfield)
56	Sidwell, Zach	OLB	6-4	225	Fr.	Kearney, Neb. (Kearney Senior)
82	Steele, Hasani	WR	5-11	170	Fr.	Glen Ellyn, Ill. (Glenbard West)
30	Stewart, Matt	FS	5-11	188	Jr.	Omaha, Neb. (Millard South)
63	Strikwerda, Nathan	OL	6-3	272	Jr.	Madison, Wis. (West)
97	Stuart, Joel	TE	6-6	220	So.	Elyria, Ohio (Catholic)
50	Sutter, Danny	ILB	6-2	225	Sr.	Peoria, Ill. (Richwoods)
25	Swenson, Jeff	WR	5-11	180	So.	Spencer, Iowa (Spencer)
97	Taylor, Gladston	DL	6-5	230	Fr.	Missouri City, Texas (Willowridge)
73	Tomkiel, Mark	OT	6-6	304	So.	Chicago, Ill. (Hubbard)
27	Valenzisi, Sam	PK	5-7	156	Sr.(5)	Westlake, Ohio (Westlake)
68	Warren, Mike	OLB	6-5	237	Sr.(5)	Antioch, Ill. (Antioch)
18	Waterman, Toussaint	WR	6-2	205	Jr.	Pontiac, Mich. (Detroit Country Day)
60	Wendland, Jason	OT	6-4	285	Sr.	Simi Valley, Calif. (Royal)
21	Wilkerson, Fred	DB	6-2	190	So.	Detroit, Mich. (Cass Tech)
64	Yeager, Larry	OL	6-3	215	Fr.	Troy, Mich. (Cranbrook Kingswood)

(5) Indicates fifth-year senior

Photo Credits

Allsport U.S.A.: 35, 52, 82-83, 88, 90, 96, 97, 99, 100-101, 102-103, 112, 113, 124, 125, 126-127, 128-129, 130-top, 130-bottom.

AP/Wide World Photo: 9, 10-11, 26-27, 73, 74-75, 76-77, 94-95, 106-107, 110-111, 118-119, 121, 145, 146, 147, 148-left, 148-149, 150, 151, 152, 153, 156.

Birmingham Post-Herald: 140-top.

Brian Bahr: Back Cover (NU students), 29, 30, 32-33, 34, 104, 108, 135.

Chris Covatta: 79.

Jonathan Daniel: Front Cover, Back Cover (Gary Barnett), 3, 12, 13, 14, 15, 16, 17, 18, 19, 20-21, 22, 24, 25, 28-top, 28-bottom, 36, 38, 39, 40, 41, 42, 43, 44-45, 46, 47, 48-49, 50, 51, 53, 54, 55, 57, 63, 65, 67, 68-69, 70-71, 81, 84-85, 87, 89, 91, 92, 93, 109, 115, 117, 118-left, 120-top, 120-bottom, 122-123, 132-133, 136, 139-bottom, 141, 143, 144.

The Detroit News: 58, 60-61, 62, 64, 66, 134.

Vincent Laforet: 37.

Northwestern University: 139-top.

Michael Scmitt: 31.

Lancaster Smith Collection: 140-bottom.

Time Inc.: 142.

Story Credits

"The Year of the Cats" has been previously published in *The Sporting News*. Reprinted by permission of Michael Wilbon.

" NU Took Advantage of Irish Mistakes" courtesy of the *Detroit Free Press*. Copyright © 1995 by the *Detroit Free Press*. Reprinted by permission.

The following stories have been reprinted courtesy of the *Los Angeles Times*. Copyright © 1995 by the *Los Angeles Times*. Reprinted by permission.
    "Dream Comes True Again for Northwestern"
    "NU's Memorable 1995 Journey Began Last Spring"

"Purple Craze" courtesy of *The Detroit News*. Copyright © 1995 by *The Detroit News*. Reprinted by permission.

The following stories have been reprinted courtesy of *The New York Times*. Copyright © 1995 by The New York Times Company. Reprinted by permission.
    "Cats Shock Irish"
    "Stopping to Smell the Roses"
    "Call it a Lost Weekend for Michigan Fans"
    "The Evanston Miracle"
    "Cats Continue to Roll"
    "One Slip Taints Wildcats' Rose Bowl Run"

The following stories have been reprinted courtesy of The Associated Press.
"What Happened to the Parade and the Parties?"
"Dashed Dreams"
"High-Flying Cats"
"The Original Believer"
"NU Routs Hoosiers"
"Reaching for the Promised Land"
"The Miracle Worker"
"Stopping a Giant"
" 'Mildcats' No More — Northwestern Has Arrived"
"New Guys on the Block"
"A Badger Bash"
"Valiant Comeback"
"Northwestern is Paterno's Kind of Team"
"Dreaming of Roses"
"Champions, Finally"
"Northwestern Takes a Drink After a Very Long Drought"
"Autry Finishes Fourth in Heisman Balloting"
"The Purple to Pasadena"
"A Journey and a Dream Falls Short"

"Wildcats' Football Success Brings Added Interest in NU" courtesy of USA Today. Copyright © 1995 Gannett Corp. Reprinted by permission.

"A Knight on the Field" courtesy of Francis J. Fitzgerald. Reprinted by permission.

"Nemeth's Sweet Smell of Roses" courtesy of the *Birmingham Post-Herald*. Copyright © 1995 by the *Birmingham Post-Herald*. Reprinted by permission.